100 INDIAN WOMEN

WHO WERE THE FIRST TO DO WHAT THEY DID

SHRUTHI RAO

Read more in the 10s series

10 Indian Animals You Will Never Again See in the Wild
by Ranjit Lal

10 Indian Monarchs Whose Amazing Stories You May Not Know
by Devika Rangachari

10 Indian Champions Who Are Fighting to Save the Planet
by Bijal Vachharajani and Radha Rangarajan

Read more by Shruthi Rao from Duckbill

Susie Will Not Speak

Manya Learns to Roar

10 INDIAN WOMEN WHO WERE THE FIRST TO DO WHAT THEY DID

SHRUTHI RAO

duckbill

An imprint of Penguin Random House

DUCKBILL BOOKS

USA | Canada | UK | Ireland | Australia
New Zealand | India | South Africa | China | Singapore

Duckbill Books is part of the Penguin Random House group of companies whose addresses can be found at global.penguinrandomhouse.com

Published by Penguin Random House India Pvt. Ltd
4th Floor, Capital Tower 1, MG Road,
Gurugram 122 002, Haryana, India

Penguin Random House India

First published by Duckbill Books 2019

This edition published in Duckbill Books by Penguin Random House India 2020

10 9 8 7 6 5 4 3 2

ISBN 9789387103207

Typeset by PrePSol Enterprises Pvt. Ltd.

Printed at Repro India Limited

10

INTRODUCTION

This book contains the stories of ten remarkable Indian women who were pioneers in their fields.

We usually encounter many of their names in answer sheets of general knowledge test banks, or as passing paragraphs in magazine articles (of course, Indira Gandhi is the clear exception here). But often, when we view their stories through the lens of the twenty-first century, without an idea of the society they lived in, we do not realise the full measure of their achievements. In this book, I have tried to describe the historical setting in which they lived and worked, and I hope the reader will be able to fathom the magnitude of the journey these women each undertook, and imagine what it must have been like to take that first step—like stepping off a cliff into the unknown!

In today's context, it seems normal that these women did what men had always done. A large part of the contribution of these women was exactly that—they made it normal for women to do anything they wanted to.

The ten women in this book are from diverse fields, and their stories are different, and so are the challenges they overcame. It is interesting to note that most of these women are clustered around the late nineteenth and early twentieth century. This coincides with the evolution of awareness of women's rights all over the world, in what is called first-wave feminism, an international movement mostly dealing with women's suffrage.

It was difficult to zero in on these ten women; there were so many contenders. Sometimes, within the span of a few years, a particular field would have multiple women entrants. Some of these women were pathbreakers not only in India but in a larger context. Take Anna Chandy—she was the first woman judge in the whole Anglo-Saxon world, decades before Britain got its first woman judge, Elizabeth Allen. But the stories of these ten were just the most compelling.

Many of the trailblazers in this book were born into privilege—and were from educated, rich or forward-thinking families. This gave them a head start over less privileged women as the financial challenges were less, and frequently, there was support at home. It was only after they stepped out into the world that patriarchy slammed doors on their faces. But others had to beat oppression, social ostracism and poverty to do what they wanted to do.

It is interesting though, that the first major sportswoman (in this book, major sportswoman is defined as the first woman to make it to an Olympic final) was winning accolades relatively recently—at the very end of the twentieth century. Many believed (and some still do) that women are inherently weak, unable to withstand the rigours of physical training, and that menstruation and pregnancy are obstacles to sporting achievements. And so, it took much longer for Indian women to take large strides in sports.

During the research for this book, I 'met' awe-inspiring women from all over the world, each of them deserving of an entire book to herself. We have these women to thank for opening up the way for all women to achieve their dreams. I hope reading about them will help you realise how much women have had to struggle to get the privileges that we have now. We must not take these for granted, any more than men should grudge us these hard-won rights.

TEACHER, THINKER, TRUTHSEEKER

Savitribai Phule

1 January 1831 – 10 March 1897

Savitribai stepped out of her house in Poona, freshly showered, the end of her sari draped over her head. She walked quickly towards the school where she was a teacher and headmistress. She was immersed in thoughts of what she would teach the children that day, when ...

Splat!

A blob of dung landed at her feet. Before she realised what was happening, another gobbet of dung flew through the air and struck her, mucking up her clean sari.

Savitribai looked around. She wasn't sure who had lobbed the dung at her, but it could be any of the dozens of people glaring at her, disapproval on their faces.

Savitribai knew why they were angry. She taught girls at her school, and in the nineteenth century, this was a big no-no. Besides, some of the girls were from the lower castes, and education for lower caste people was taboo too.

How dare this woman, herself from a lower caste, challenge the strict rules of society?

But Savitribai wasn't one to be perturbed by mere dung-flinging. 'I'm just doing my duty,' she called out to the people around her. 'May god bless you and forgive you.' She marched on to her school.

The same thing happened the following day. And the next. The day after that, Savitribai walked to school in an old sari, and changed into a fresh one at school. In the evening, she changed back into the dung-smeared sari and walked home.

Such was the calm conviction with which Savitribai lived her life, in the face of constant opposition from the section of society whose authority she challenged. A scholar, writer, social reformer, and an advocate of women's rights and liberation, she was the first woman teacher of India, and one of the first women in the country to get her work published. Along with her husband, the social revolutionary Jotirao Phule, Savitribai bravely led a lifelong crusade on behalf of India's oppressed people.

India in the ninteenth century had a rigid caste structure, much, much worse than it is now. The story often doled out to us is that the caste system was created by divine intervention, dividing people on the lines of the work they do. All harmless and above board, you see.

But the reality was quite different. The upper castes, with their access to education, created the rules to suit themselves. They kept the lower castes and Dalits, considered lower than the lowest castes, oppressed, so that they could continue meekly to provide the labour necessary for the economy to function and for the upper castes to live in comfort.

Only upper-caste children, primarily boys, were allowed access to schools. Education was dangerous; reading and writing could make people aware of the unfairness of the caste system, give them access to more economic options and lead them to rebel against the upper castes.

Women were also denied access to education, by and large, regardless of caste and social class. Their role was to stay at home and provide free and unacknowledged labour and services. Even social reformers of that time, like Bal Gangadhar Tilak, were opposed to education of women.

While there were social reform movements like the Brahmo Samaj and Arya Samaj, they were confined to the upper castes. There was no large-scale, consolidated movement against the upper-caste hegemony.

This was the kind of India that Savitri was born into.

The girl who asked questions

Savitri was a curious child and constantly asked her mother questions, until her mother had to frogmarch her out of the kitchen. Savitri was fearless too. Once, her friend, who was sitting on a tree, refused to come down because a snake had slithered onto the branch below him. Savitri moved the snake to a different branch, and helped the friend down.

When Savitri was nine years old, her parents got her married to Jotirao Phule, who was thirteen.

Jotirao was from a shudra (lower caste) family, and ordinarily he would not have been allowed anywhere near a school. But two of his neighbours were teachers, and they noticed how intelligent the young boy was. One was Muslim and the other Christian, so they probably didn't subscribe to rules about not educating lower-caste children. They persuaded his father to send him to a mission school, where Jotirao came to admire the discipline and conviction of his teachers.

Jotirao read widely, including books on the lives of Martin Luther, George Washington and Shivaji. He was especially impressed by *The Rights of Man* by Thomas Paine, a political activist, writer and philosopher. Jotirao absorbed ideas about the equality of all humans.

Jotirao became aware that women had no access to education. And he knew that the best way to empower women and see that they enjoyed full human rights, was through education. He felt that unless the state of women was improved, the country wouldn't be able to progress. As the first step, he set about educating Savitri.

There were a few schools for girls in India, run by Christian missionaries, especially in Calcutta (Kolkata). But not too many girls attended those schools, possibly because people were slightly wary of missionaries. There were no schools for girls run by Indians or by the government.

> In 1847, Peary Charan Sarkar, a government school headmaster, and Bengali educator, Kalikrishna Mitra set up a free school for girls in Barasat (later named Kalikrishna Girls' High School).

The Phules decided to start one. Savitri and another woman, Fatima Sheikh, went to Mrs Farrar's Academy in Ahmednagar and 'Normal School' (which is what teacher training schools were called) in Poona for training.. They may have been the first Indian women to be trained as teachers.

Cynthia Farrar was an American missionary, who was a superintendent of girls' schools in India. She also taught teachers, and her schools had 400 Indian girls studying, in spite of local opposition.

Schools for girls

In 1848, the Phules opened a school in Bhidewada, Poona, with nine girls. Savitri and Fatima were the teachers, and Savitri was also the headmistress. She was seventeen years old at the time.

People were incensed. Teaching women? Teaching lower castes? And grouping girls of all castes together in the classroom? Would the horrors never cease?

The couple was harassed and abused. When threats and dung and stones didn't stop Savitri, people went to Jotirao's father and filled his ears with tales of how his son was going against religious precepts. Jotirao's father threw Savitri and Jotirao out of his home.

The young couple packed up and went to live on their own.

By this time, word had spread about the school. People came forward to donate funds, supplies and books. Another building was found—Fatima Sheikh's father's house—and a second school started in 1851.

Contemporary government school committee reports on the Phules' school gushed about how happy the girls were in the school, and how the prejudices against women's education were being removed. A year later, the education department of the British government felicitated the Phules in a public ceremony.

The Phules opened several more schools, boarding schools and hostels, and started literacy classes for adults too.

> 'The number of girl students in Jotirao's school is ten times more than the number of boys studying in the government schools. This is because the system of teaching girls is far superior to what is available for boys in government schools. ... If the Government Education Board does not do something about this soon, seeing these women outshine the men will make us hang our heads in shame'—*Poona Observer* (29 May 1852)

An ideal society

The Phules dreamt of building a society without discrimination. It was an audacious dream, and it required immense courage to try to bring it about. One of the most outrageous things the Phules did was to open up the well in their house for the use of Dalits.

Once, while recovering from an illness at her mother's house in Naigaon, Savitri became aware of a commotion on the streets. A brahmin man and a shudra woman had fallen in love, and their relationship had just become public. An inter-caste relationship? Scandal! Sacrilege! A mob had dragged the couple to the streets, surrounded them and closed in, weapons raised.

Savitri elbowed into the group of people, looked them in their murderous eyes, and talked them down. She promised to send the couple away from the city.

The mob let the couple go. Savitri sent them to her husband in Poona, who made arrangements for their livelihood.

Savitri started a women's association called Mahila Seva Mandal in 1852. She educated women about their rights as humans, and gave lectures to raise people's awareness of the plight of women and the unfair treatment many of them received.

At this time, widows were considered impure, and treated as social outcastes. Since child marriage was common, many widows were young girls destined to spend their entire lives in austerity, in thankless service of others. Widows were sometimes forced into abusive relationships, and abandoned when they became pregnant. The fate of such widows, and the children born to them, was unimaginably heartbreaking. One story which received media attention decades later, in 1881, was that of a brahmin widow Vijayalakshmi who killed her newborn and was sentenced to death. But there were many such stories.

Savitri established a shelter in her own house for pregnant widows. She looked after them, assisted them with the delivery, and even brought up their children. She encouraged widows to remarry, and organised a barbers' strike against the terribly humiliating custom of shaving the heads of widows.

The Phules adopted the son of a pregnant brahmin widow, whom they saved from suicide. Yashwant later became a doctor, and was actively involved in the social reform activities of his parents.

The Phules founded the Satyashodhak Samaj (Society of Truthseekers). Its objective was 'to redeem shudras and atishudras (those who don't belong to any caste/Dalits) from the influence of the brahmanical scriptures, teach them their human rights and liberate them from mental and religious slavery.' The Satyashodhaks fought for social justice, and tried to build a society that would do away with caste and social barriers. They campaigned for universal education, and protested against the tyranny of upper castes.

Savitribai headed the women's unit of the Satyashodhak Samaj, and later, after Jotirao's death, the entire Samaj. She was in charge of its day-to-day activities, and led Satyashodhaks on many campaigns. The Samaj arranged weddings without a brahmin presiding (which was unheard of then, and is still rare). The new couples had to take an oath to support education and equality.

When Jotirao died in 1890, Yashwant was about to perform the funeral rites, but a cousin protested, saying that Yashwant wasn't a blood relative and did not have the right. This was a valid objection according to contemporary social norms. In response, Yashwant raised an objection to the suggestion that the cousin should perform the rites.

Savitri stepped forward and lit the pyre herself. This sent shock waves through society. It was said that a man needed a son, for who else would light his funeral pyre? Savitri had shown an alternative.

Savitribai's beliefs and actions are striking even today. In her time, her ideas caused extreme anger and ire. But she was undaunted.

When famine struck Maharashtra in 1896, Savitribai raised money, organised supplies, and assisted the affected farmers, along with Satyashodhak volunteers. She established hostels for children orphaned by the famine and fed thousands of people.

Farmers were particularly vulnerable due to the failure of their crops. Moneylenders took advantage by charging high interest rates for loans. The Satyashodhaks, while providing relief to the farmers, advised them against borrowing from the moneylenders. In retaliation, the moneylenders complained to the police that the Satyashodhaks were causing riots and got them arrested.

Savitribai marched to the district collector and brought this to his attention. The collector admonished the moneylenders, released the Satyashodhaks, and himself got involved in relief efforts, sending truckloads of food to the affected.

Savitribai once again plunged into relief work the following year, when the plague hit Maharashtra. She nursed the sick without any thought to her own health. She contracted the plague while carrying a sick child to the doctor, and died.

Literary work

Savitribai was one of the first Indian women to be published, and is considered a pioneer of modern Marathi poetry.

In *Kavya Phule*, she used the abhang form of folk poetry and simple and effective language, to write about nature, education and the caste system, asking people to shed the shackles of slavery. Another collection, *Bavan Kashi Subodh Ratnakar*, was a biography of Jotirao Phule in verse.

She also published two collections of her own speeches, as well as a collection of some speeches by Jotirao.

'I have not seen another woman as kind and loving as Savitribai. She gave us more love than even a mother could'—Laxman Karadi Jaaya in a student memoir

SOME CONTEMPORARY INDIAN WOMEN SOCIAL REFORMERS

Pandita Ramabai (1858–1922) was a scholar, educator and feminist, who lectured internationally on women's liberation and rights, and established women's shelters and schools in India.

Tarabai Shinde (1850–1910) was a women's rights activist whose *Stri Purush Tulana (Comparison between Man and Woman)*, published in 1881, is considered to be India's first feminist work.

Ramabai Ranade (1863–1924) was a social reformer, who established and led the women's wing of the Arya Samaj, headed Seva Sadan, which was involved in the education and training of thousands of women, and worked in prison and hospital reform.

AROUND THE WORLD

Laura Bassi (1711–1778) was the first woman professor in the world, of Anatomy and Philosophy in Bologna and the chair of experimental physics at the Institute of Sciences, Bologna.

Emma Willard (1787–1870) was an American educationist, who started the Troy Female Seminary in 1821, the first higher education institution for women in the USA.

Maria Montessori (1870–1952) was one of Italy's first woman doctors and a pioneer in a pedagogy that is still used the world over.

A DOCTOR FOR WOMEN

Kadambini Ganguly

18 July 1861 – 23 October 1923

Imagine being a woman in nineteenth-century India, where social conditioning made women reluctant to talk to men who were not part of the family. If you suffered from a health problem that required you to go to a doctor (who were all men), you might prefer to die a painful death. Or worse, imagine that you are willing to go, but your family would rather let you die (a painful death) than let a man examine you.

Hundreds of women, especially those who lived in seclusion, died needlessly because they didn't have access to women doctors.

This was the main reason why the medical profession in India opened its doors to women in the nineteenth century, even when female literacy was as low as one per cent. In contrast, the first women lawyers, engineers and civil servants made their appearance well into the twentieth century. India was among the first countries in the world where women could get medical degrees.

'Women doctors? What for?'

In the late 1800s, there had been discussions in educated circles in India about the need for women doctors. But many people said that it was enough if India just trained more midwives (who help during childbirth). Okay, they said, if you insist, then the midwives can be trained in women's health problems. After all, what else do we need women in the medical profession for, if not to deal with childbirth? It is not like women doctors will ever treat men!

Christian missionaries in India were among the first to realise the need for women doctors. Some missionaries got basic training and helped out. Dr Clara Swain was the first woman doctor to come to India from the US. She opened a dispensary in Bareilly, trained women and treated patients. Many more American women doctors followed. Once Britain opened up the field for women in their own country, British doctors started arriving too.

When Mary Scharlieb of Britain accompanied her barrister husband to Madras (Chennai) in 1866, she quickly realised the need for women medical professionals. She took a midwifery course but wasn't satisfied. She constantly pressured the educational authorities to train women in medicine. Finally, in 1875, Mary and three other women, all European or Anglo-Indian, joined Madras Medical College. This was a year before Britain opened up the medical profession to women.

Mary and the others got their LMS (Licentiate in Medicine and Surgery) degrees in 1878. Mary went to England for higher studies, and practised and taught both in India and England.

Calcutta Medical College had been receiving applications from Indian women, but the authorities had dilly-dallied about taking a decision. They finally stated they would admit only women who had BA degrees.

They didn't have to wait long.

'Women are unfitted for the medical profession which demands physical power and endurance, cool judgement and strong nerves—qualities in which women are specially deficient'—letter from a council member of the Calcutta Medical College to the officiating principal (11 May 1882)

Making history

Kadambini was born at a time when society was simmering with change. Since the First War of Independence in 1857, a new social and political awareness fuelled many movements all over India.

One such was the Brahmo Samaj. Started in 1828 by Raja Ram Mohan Roy as a movement to reform Hinduism, it denounced caste system, superstition, polytheism and image worship. In 1861, a branch broke off to focus on social reform. It encouraged the education of women, remarriage of widows and abolition of child marriage. Members of the Brahmo Samaj were called Brahmos.

Banga Mahila Vidyalaya, where Kadambini studied, was started in 1875 by a group of Brahmos, along with Annette Akroyd, an Englishwoman who believed in the equality of sexes. The girls of Banga Mahila Vidyalay studied subjects that weren't ordinarily taught to women because it would 'tax their brains', like arithmetic, geography, politics, physical science, history and English, apart from music, dancing, etiquette, needlework and practical housework.

In 1878, Kadambini cleared the entrance examination of the University of Calcutta, the first woman to do so. The department of education of the government of Bengal showered her with awards: a monthly scholarship of Rs 15 and a book stipend of a whopping Rs 50 for higher studies.

But how would she utilise this scholarship? There was nothing in Calcutta at that time for women. Then Bethune College started First Arts classes, and Kadambini cleared those examinations too.

Kadambini knew she wanted to study medicine. But she would need a BA. Same problem again. Where would she study? Back went Bethune College to the authorities, and got permission and funds to start BA classes for women.

Kadambini joined the BA classes, as did Chandramukhi Bose, who had cleared the First Arts examination from Dehradun Native Christian School. The two women made history when they received their BA degrees in 1882, becoming the first women graduates in India.

Chandramukhi Bose went on to become the first woman in India to get an MA degree. Later, she became the first woman principal of an undergraduate college (Bethune) in the whole of south Asia!

Kadambini Ganguly applied to Calcutta Medical College and the college was forced to accept her. She started classes in June 1883. Not much is known about her years in college, but when she took the examinations in 1887, she failed in one subject. It is suggested in some sources that the instructor-in-charge wasn't happy about the idea of women doctors, and failed her.

The principal of the college, Dr Coates, said he wouldn't be able to confer the MB (Bachelor in Medicine) degree on her, but offered her the GBMC (Graduate of Bengal Medical College) degree. And Kadambini became the first woman licenced to practise medicine in India.

Taking on many challenges

In 1883, Kadambini married social reformer Dwarakanath Ganguly, who had been her teacher at school. He was a widower with children, the eldest of whom wasn't much younger than Kadambini.

While Kadambini was still doing her medical degree, she gave birth to children. It was believed that when a woman entered a profession as demanding as this, she wouldn't be able to have a domestic life at all, and here was Kadambini proving this wrong!

> 'This young lady, Mrs Ganguly, married! after she made up her mind to become a doctor! and has had one, if not two children since. But she was absent only thirteen days for her lying-in!! and did not miss, I believe, a single lecture!!'—Florence Nightingale in a letter to a friend (20 February 1888)

Kadambini raised eight children (including those from her husband's first marriage) and somehow found the time to handmake fine lace while commuting in horse-drawn carriages from one patient's home to another.

In 1885, the Lady Dufferin Fund (also known as the National Association for Supplying Female Medical Aid to the Women of India) had been set up to encourage the establishment of maternity hospitals and baby clinics in India, and the Lady Dufferin Women's Hospital was a result of that fund.

Kadambini joined this hospital as a doctor, with a monthly salary of Rs 300, then a very large amount. All the higher-level responsibilities were given only to European doctors. Kadambini's jobs were equivalent to those of nurses and midwives. She was frustrated, and said that she was even ready to work without salary if she were given the charge of a full ward at the hospital. But the authorities refused. If that happened, Kadambini would be an equal colleague of white doctors and that would never do, would it?

'It is a recognised fact ... that the performance of hospital duties quietly improve the qualifications of a doctor ... without giving Indian medical women opportunities to prove their capabilities, it is not fair to them to pronounce that they are not competent to hold first-class appointments and to be placed in responsible charge of large and important hospitals'—Kadambini in a letter to a newspaper (*c.*1889)

There were other challenges as well. It was assumed, as it still often is even in the twenty-first century, that greater liberty equals loss of 'virtue'. In 1891, *Bangabasi* newspaper published an article, in which Kadambini was called a prostitute, and the Brahmo Samaj slapped them with a case of libel. The editor of *Bangabasi* had pay a fine of Rs 100 and was sentenced to prison for six months.

In 1893, Kadambini travelled to the UK to study further. Newspaper reports say that by this time, she had also passed the LMS examinations in India.

Kadambini passed what was known as the Triple Qualifications Examination. She obtained three diplomas: Licentiate of the College of Physicians, Edinburg (LRCP), Licentiate of the College of Surgeons, Glasgow (LRCS), and Licentiate of the Faculty of Physicians and Surgeons, Dublin (LFPS). She came back with recommendations from famous doctors and Lady Dufferin (of the hospital fame) herself.

It took the weight of foreign qualifications to give her the dignity she deserved. She became the superintendent of Lady Dufferin Hospital and joined Eden Female Hospital as outdoor physician. Plus, she was appointed to give lectures to the women students of Campbell Medical School, which had by this time started admitting women. This was one of the first instances where an Indian woman was asked to teach students at such a high level.

Along with this, Kadambini also involved herself in the politics and concerns of the day. She was one of the first women to attend a session of the Indian National Congress in Bombay (Mumbai) in 1889. In 1890, at the Calcutta session, she gave the vote of thanks, becoming the first woman to speak at a session of the INC. She also organised meetings, collected funds and raised awareness about several oppressed groups, from Indian workers in South Africa to the labourers of the tea gardens of Assam and the coal mines of Bihar.

Carrying on the battle

Kadambini left her government job and started private practice. The Nepal royal family was among her patients. In one instance, she saved the queen mother who was close to death, and the grateful royal family plied her with money, expensive ornaments and artefacts. They even gave her a pony, which her children and step-grandchildren enjoyed thoroughly! She treated the poor for free, and also worked with women in seclusion.

In a case that made her famous, male doctors had given up on a woman saying that she had an inoperable tumour, but Kadambini diagnosed it as—wait for it—pregnancy! The woman delivered a healthy child.

In spite of her growing fame, many people still refused to see her as a doctor. They saw her as a dai or a midwife, asking her to do all the cleaning up duties too, which ordinarily midwives do. But Kadambini didn't let herself be affected.

On the morning of the day Kadambini died in 1923, she conducted a complicated surgery on a patient, and commented to her daughter-in-law with pride, 'They say that Dr Ganguly has become aged. If they saw the operation I did today, they wouldn't dare make that remark!'

SOME OTHER PIONEERING INDIAN WOMEN DOCTORS

The first Indian women to get LMS degrees from Madras Medical College were **Abala Das**, **Rose Govindarajulu** and **Gurdial Singh**. This was in 1888, a few months after Kadambini got her licence. Abala Das didn't practise, but went on to become a social activist and married scientist JC Bose. Rose Govindarajulu (1865–1921) got advanced degrees from Scotland, Ireland and Brussels and had a remarkable career as a doctor in Mysore Medical Mission, where she opened a number of maternity hospitals. **Annie Jagannathan** also started in Madras Medical College around the same time, but moved to Edinburgh to continue her studies. She died in 1894.

Anandibai Joshi (1865–1887) got her MD degree in Pennsylvania, US in 1886, and became the first Indian woman to qualify as a doctor. She worked briefly at the Albert Edward Hospital in Kolhapur.

Rukhmabai (1864–1965) who famously petitioned Queen Victoria to annul her child marriage, graduated in 1894 from London School of Medicine for Women, and went on to work as chief medical officer at a hospital in Surat.

AROUND THE WORLD

Dorothea Erxleben (1715–1762) is the first woman in the world recorded as getting a modern medical degree.

James Barry (1789–1865; born Margaret Ann Bulkley but possibly transgender) got a medical degree in Edinbugh in 1812 and worked as an army doctor.

Marie Duchover (1809–1893) was of French origin but got a medical degree in Rio de Janeiro in 1824 and practised medicine in Brazil for over sixty years.

THE LAW IN HER OWN HANDS

Cornelia Sorabji

15 November 1866 – 6 July 1954

Little Cornelia was lying on her tummy, reading, when a visitor arrived at their home in Poona to see her mother. Cornelia later said that this visitor 'set my own feet on the path that I have chosen.'

Cornelia stopped reading, to listen to the conversation. The woman's husband had died. Since she was a purdahnashin (a woman who lived in seclusion and didn't show herself to men not related to her), she was forced to depend on a manager to manage her property. She gave him verbal instructions through a screen, and signed blank papers, trusting him to do the right thing. But the manager cheated her. Over her signature on one of the blank sheets, he wrote out a statement transferring her entire wealth to himself.

> 'I had crept to my Mother's knee, while the Thakurani was speaking, and when she had gone, my Mother said to me, "Did you understand what she said?"
> "Only that she is in great trouble," said I (as my Mother reminded me in later years), "and even you cannot help her."

"That is so," said my Mother. "There are many Indian women in trouble in that way. Would you like to learn how to help them?"
I said, "Oh! I should!"
"Then, when you grow up and are able to choose the special thing you want to learn, ask to study the Law. That will show you the way to help in this kind of trouble."
And that was her secret and mine, fostered openly from time to time, when we talked of careers. I was going to be a Lawyer'—Cornelia in *India Calling*

Cornelia set her sights on becoming a lawyer at a time when law was exclusively a male domain.

'A way will open'

Cornelia's parents brought up their children to be self-reliant, and take their own decisions. Whenever there was a choice to be made, be it in the clothes they wore or the profession they would choose, they told their children, 'It is your puzzle, you must solve it.'

Cornelia's mother, Francina, was of the Toda tribe of the Nilgiris, and raised by an English couple. Cornelia's father, Sorabji Kharsedji, was born a Parsi but converted to Christianity and became a missionary. Both were deeply invested in education, especially women's education. Francina started a number of schools, and her house was open to women looking for advice and help. The family had many friends in the English community, both in India and in England, and some of them provided invaluable support when Cornelia faced difficulties pursuing her higher education.

Cornelia and her siblings were tutored at home, and taught languages, mathematics, music and drawing.

There were no women's colleges near Poona, but Cornelia figured out that there was nothing stopping her from asking for admission at a men's college. And so, she joined Deccan College, Poona. She topped the university in the final degree examinations, and graduated with a BA in 1887, becoming the first Indian woman in western India to get a university degree, five years after Kadambini Ganguly and Chandramukhi Bose got their degrees.

She instantly became an inspiration. Three women joined Bombay university the very next year after they heard about Cornelia's success in the examination.

Since Cornelia topped the examination, she became eligible for a generous government of India scholarship to study at an English university, including travelling expenses. But the authorities refused to grant her the scholarship, because their opinion about higher education abroad for women was that 'It is nonsense for a woman to even think about it.'

Her parents said, 'Hard luck! But the goal is still there. A way will open!' Their attitude probably rubbed off on Cornelia and kept her going all through her life.

Cornelia was offered a temporary teaching position in English literature in a college in Gujarat. She was the only woman on the entire campus, an eighteen-year-old in a men's college. It was, in her words, 'solitary and (inwardly) terrifying'. But she enjoyed the experience and the responsibilities, and discovered her ability to make quick decisions.

Cornelia's story about being denied the scholarship bothered more than just her immediate family. Their family friends and well-wishers put forth an appeal for funds in the London

Times. They extolled Cornelia's achievements and capabilities, and that she was in need of money to study in England.

The appeal was a success, and the money poured in. Notable people (including Florence Nightingale) contributed funds, and Cornelia's dream came alive again.

Blazing trails at Oxford

Cornelia sailed to Oxford in 1889. At first, she was advised to study English literature, because she had funding for a two-year course, and a law course would last three years. Besides, everyone considered literature a more suitable subject for a woman.

But after a year, Cornelia decided to study for the Bachelor of Civil Laws degree, the highest legal course in Oxford. She knew she wouldn't receive a degree, since Oxford wouldn't grant women degrees (this changed only in 1920), though women had been allowed to study since 1879. Cornelia wouldn't even be able to practise law, because the legal profession was exclusively male. But with such a qualification, she thought, she would be in a better position to negotiate her way through the field of law.

The vice-chancellor, Benjamin Jowett admitted her to the law school as a special case. She became the first woman ever to study for the BCL at Oxford.

The professors arranged special lectures for her to make up for what she'd missed in the first year. Cornelia was also permitted to enter the Codrington Library, which was off-limits for women. The warden was so impressed with her hard work that when other women asked if they could get entry to the library too, he joked, 'Certainly, if you can prove that you are Miss Sorabji!'

Cornelia rubbed shoulders with members of parliament, authors, poets, artistes and the leading luminaries of the day. Her time in Oxford was the happiest in her life. She worked hard, studied hard, was intellectually satisfied, and socially welcome. There were of course some dons who treated her patronizingly, and seemed surprised by 'her intellect and quickness of perception'. One teacher said 'she managed to do better' than her male classmates. But for Cornelia, these were minor blips, and she ignored them.

In 1892, Cornelia appeared for the exams (in spite of the external examiners refusing to examine a woman) and became the first woman to pass Oxford's BCL exams. She would have to wait for more than thirty years to be awarded a formal degree, though.

A career in law

Cornelia did a six-month apprenticeship with a solicitor's firm in London called Lee and Pemberton. After her return to Bombay, she took up chamber counselling in matters related to women's property, and worked as a consultant for women clients at a Parsi solicitors' firm, though women clients were scarce.

Meanwhile, she was also appointed the commissioner of education by the Gaekwad of Baroda, and she had to travel around his principality and evaluate the schools. But she felt she wasn't making use of her legal education.

Cornelia really wanted to plead cases in court. In 1896, an opportunity came up to defend a woman accused of murder. Since the case was to be heard in the sessions court, Cornelia knew she could argue the case 'as a person for the defence of the accused'. The High Court was consulted. They were surprised to note that they had left women this loophole, but conceded that they couldn't stop Cornelia.

Cornelia says, 'The week of the trial was, without comparison, the most exciting and the most exhausting of my entire life.' And she won the case decisively.

But getting into the higher courts was an uphill task. Cornelia wanted to work at the Bombay High Court. She took the LLB examination from Bombay University in 1897. This qualified her to work as a vakil, one grade lower than a barrister. But Bombay High Court refused, saying, 'Can you cite a precedence of a woman vakil?' She couldn't. She couldn't even come up with the name of another law student.

She decided to try Ahmedabad High Court. She cleared the high court pleaders' examination in 1899. But Ahmedabad High Court gave her this lofty and subservient reason: 'It would be impertinent of an Indian High Court to admit women to its rolls before England had given the lead.'

The purdahnashins

The original reason Cornelia had wanted to study law was for the purdahnashins. She knew they needed legal help, and she was the only person who could give it. Purdahnashins were women, both Hindu and Muslim, who wore the purdah (veil) and spent their lives in seclusion. They weren't allowed to communicate with the outside world directly, but only through husbands and close male relatives.

Cornelia's focus was, in particular, towards widowed purdahnashins. Such women had to appoint a manager to look after all their affairs, talk to these men through curtains and sign blank documents. They had little knowledge or control over what these managers were doing, and could easily be taken advantage of. The irony was that if the women wanted to complain against their manager, they had to send the complaint through the same manager.

Some of these women and their children belonged to the Court of Wards, which the British set up to manage the affairs of those estates whose owners had died, and whose heirs were still minors, or if there was some other problem. There were guardians in charge of each estate, and lawyers to oversee their legal affairs, but all of them were men, and had to communicate with the purdahnashins through screens. Sometimes, these guardians weren't even sure if they were speaking to the right woman!

Cornelia felt that if a woman could be appointed as an advisor in the Court of Wards, then she could meet the purdahnashins in person, and many of these problems would be solved. She wrote to viceroys, politicians, and judges, and legal representatives both in England and India. She wrote letters to newspapers in England, and articles highlighting the plight of the purdahnashins. She toured India, giving lectures on the topic, and talking to any authority who would listen.

Finally, in 1904, the British government approved Cornelia's request and she became the first woman legal adviser of the Court of Wards, and the first Indian woman to occupy a senior bureaucratic role in the British empire.

For Cornelia, this was a double victory. Not only would she be working with purdahnashins, but the legal field in India had finally recognised the presence of a woman!

For nearly twenty years, Cornelia worked with the purdahnashins of Bengal, helping over 600 women and children. She became their confidante, managed their affairs, and succeeded in solving problems that had been troubling them for years. Once the government realised the kind of relationship Cornelia had with them, they even sought her help to deal with some estates that were considered 'troublesome' and uncooperative—she spoke to the women of these estates, mediated between them and the government, and brought about fair agreements.

Cornelia became extremely fond of purdahnashins, and considered them family. The purdahnashins and everybody in their establishments loved and respected Cornelia as well. Cornelia went beyond what was officially required of her, travelled long distances to meet them, and got involved in the most intricate aspects of the lives of the women she interacted with. She gave them help, comfort, and a kind, listening ear. She organised gatherings where women in purdah could come together and meet others of their own kind.

'Across country I've travelled in palanquins, on elephants, in the quaintest of ancient carrying-chairs and carriages; I've been offered every kind of beast to ride and drive; and in later years, motor cars in every stage of dilapidation. I became expert in riding elephants without fatigue, sitting close up behind the mahout'—Cornelia in *India Calling*

She also used her influence with purdahnashins to make them change their ways of living, health and hygiene. She saved properties from being lost, and prevented money-motivated murders. She arranged for education for young children, so that they would grow up literate and aware of their rights.

Cornelia spoke about how intelligent and fiery some purdahnashins were. She developed a great admiration for them, and wrote extensively about them and their individual cases in her memoirs and books.

Finally, a barrister!

In 1921, women in India acquired the right to plead before the courts of law. Cornelia registered herself as a vakil in Ahmedabad High Court. In 1923, the Legal Practitioners' (Women) Act was passed, formally removing the ban on women from practising law in India. Cornelia went to England to finally and formally receive the BCL degree. She was also called to the bar from Lincoln's Inn in April 1923.

However, she never actually got to argue cases in court—again because of the discrimination against women.

Cornelia had to fight long battles with the government for years, for an increase in her pay, for the right official titles, since she was neither English nor male. She was often paid less than her male colleagues, and sometimes, she wasn't paid at all.

Her male colleagues didn't want to appear opposite her in court, because they didn't want to lose face by losing to a woman. So they conspired to keep her out of court. Some spread rumours that she didn't want work, and if she lost a case, they said it is because 'women don't know the law'. The newspapers reported only her failures. Sometimes, clients approached her for initial consultation, and hired male lawyers who would utilise the advice she had given the clients.

Both in England and India, lawyers had their own networks for contacts and work. Cornelia didn't have anything like that, firstly, because of her gender, and secondly, because she didn't fit culturally in either place. Besides, the aggressiveness in the courts, lack of morality and disrespect towards women plaintiffs made her angry and disillusioned.

'These make one tired through and through,' she wrote to a friend. But then, she also wrote: 'One could not waste time either on resentment or on a fight.' And that's what kept her going.

Cornelia always felt like an outsider wherever she went. In India, she was too much like an Englishwoman to fit in. In England, her attire and brown skin made her stand apart. In the Parsi community, she was treated as a Christian. In the Christian community, her Parsi roots were too obvious. In her profession of course, she stood out for her gender. Her support for British rule in the era of the independence movement, has also made her a somewhat problematic figure.

One person was her constant friend and confidant: Elena Rathbone, whom she had met in college. Cornelia wrote letters to Elena regularly about everything that happened to her, and about her feelings. Thanks to these letters, we know so much about the troubles Cornelia went through, and how she felt about them!

Cornelia wrote short stories, articles and letters to newspapers. Her two autobiographical works are *India Calling: The Memories of Cornelia Sorabji* and *India Recalled*. Some of her other books include *Love and Life Beyond the Purdah*, *Sun-Babies: Studies in the Child-life of India*, *Between the Twilights* (an account of some of her legal cases) and *The Purdahnashin*. She also wrote a memoir of her parents and of her sister Susie, an educationist.

Cornelia spent the last ten years of her life in England. She had started losing her eyesight as early as 1919, and it steadily deteriorated. She died of pneumonia on 6 July 1954.

'She travelled up and down the country like some knight-errant of old, rescuing distressed damsels, and bringing justice and succour to lonely women who had no other reliable helper. She travelled by every kind of conveyance—boat, train, elephant and palanquin. She crossed flooded rivers or camped under the stars in sandy wastes. Always she must be on the move, even when fever or weariness demanded rest'— Cornelia's obituary in *Glasgow Herald*

OTHER INDIAN WOMEN IN LAW

Mithan Tata (1898–1981) was India's first woman barrister, who was called to the English bar in 1923. She practised at the Bombay High Court for three years, later taught law at the Law College, Bombay, and helped amend the Parsi Marriage and Divorce Act (1936).

Anna Chandy (1905–1996) became the first woman judge in India in 1937, and the first woman High Court judge in 1959.

Leila Seth (1930–2017) became the first woman Chief Justice of a High Court in India in 1991.

AROUND THE WORLD

Marija Milutinović Punktatorka (1810–1875) graduated with a law degree and practised from *c*.1847 in Serbia.

Arabella Mansfield (1846–1911) was the first US woman to be admitted to the bar in Iowa in 1869, but she didn't practise law.

Ada H. Kepley (1847–1925) was the US woman to graduate with a law degree in 1870, but she was only allowed to practise from 1881.

Anna Yevreinova (1844–1919) was Russian but got a law degree in Germany in 1873 (the first woman to get a law degree in that country).

Eliza Orme (1848–1937) was the first UK woman to get a law degree in 1888, but she was not admitted to the bar. The first British woman to become a barrister was **Ivy Williams** in 1921.

THE POWER OF PEACEFUL PROTEST

Anasuya Sarabhai

11 November 1885 – 11 September 1972

The first ever organised strike of factory workers in India was coordinated by Anasuya Sarabhai. She also established and led the first trade union in the country, when she organised the workers in the cotton and textile mills at Ahmedabad in the early 1900s.

> A trade or labour union is an association of workers, especially in a factory or a workplace. Through creating a collective workers try to safeguard their rights, and improve their salaries and working conditions.

What is unusual is that Anasuya was not one of the mill workers. In fact, she was from a family of mill owners.

Anasuya had a privileged childhood. Her father was the owner of Calico Mills in Ahmedabad, and theirs was a rich and prosperous business family. She went to the best schools. Horse-drawn carriages ferried her to music and piano lessons, and to the houses of British acquaintances so that she could learn conversational English. Anasuya learnt interior decoration, gardening and table manners. She did well at her studies, and was an adored child.

When Anasuya was nine, her parents died within a few months of each other. Her uncle was now her guardian. As was the custom, he got Anasuya married when she was thirteen.

But the boy that Anasuya married was failing his school examinations, while Anasuya was one of the better students. How would it look if a wife did better at school than her husband? What if that embarrassed him? So they pulled Anasuya out of school.

Anasuya didn't like this. Nor was she happy at her husband's home. Her husband apparently abused her, and her brother Ambalal brought his sister back to the family home.

Anasuya studied by herself, and read extensively. She was drawn to religion, meditation and spirituality, and considered Swami Vivekananda her spiritual guide. Inspired by the need to help people, she decided to become a Jain sadhvi. At this time, she met one Dr Erulkar, who urged her to give up these ideas of retiring from worldly life. 'Go to London to study medicine and qualify as a doctor. There are hardly any lady doctors in India. On your return, you will be able to serve better the cause of women and the downtrodden!'

To London—and back

Anasuya cleared the London matriculation exam and started her studies. She lived in a vegetarian hostel, frequented the theatre and attended lectures by Indian patriots.

But one day, she passed a butcher's shop and saw the carcass of a calf hanging from a nail. She was disturbed by the sight, and the realisation hit her that if she continued studying medicine, she would be required to dissect dead bodies.

She switched to sociology at the London School of Economics. This was a time in London when the suffragettes and Fabians were active. She learned about women's struggle for equal rights, the conditions of the working class and the history of their struggles.

Suffragettes: Women who sought the right to vote, through organised protests.

Fabians: Members of a group who believed in moving to a socialist society in a gradual, evolved way, rather than with sudden revolution, as Marxists believed.

Socialist society: A society where the businesses and industries are controlled by the community or by the government (and not by a few wealthy people), leading to a more equitable distribution of wealth.

As Anasuya got more involved in these exciting political ideas, she received news that her sister Kumudkishore had died of tuberculosis. Anasuya abandoned her studies and rushed back to India, fully aware that this would be the end of her formal education.

Ambalal had been in charge of the family's factories for a while now, and he was both wealthy and influential. He welcomed Anasuya's return.

The family home had extensive gardens and grounds. Ambalal lived in the main house, and Anasuya lived in a modest building in the same compound. She dressed in plain white saris, but stopped covering her hair, and rode in open carriages, both rather bold for her time.

Changing lives

Near the textile mills outside Delhi Gate in Ahmedabad stood the Amarpura chawls, where mill workers lived. These buildings were overcrowded, and sanitation and hygiene standards were non-existent. There were lots of children, and some of them, as young as nine, worked in the mills too. (Contemporary labour laws said that twelve-year-olds could work full time, and children between nine and twelve were allowed to work half days.) Whether they worked in the mills or not, there was no question of education for them.

Aghast at this state of affairs, Anasuya and her friend Jashodabehn decided to start a school for the children near the chawls in March 1914. The challenge was, however, to get the kids to come to school.

'We noticed before us emaciated and despondent children, their bodies naked and covered with dirt and unkempt hair. We commenced our work in right earnest. We would bathe them and comb their hair after applying oil when innumerable lice would come out. While carrying out the washing of hair we had to wear an apron. We got clothes stitched from our curtains in our home—and thus a small beginning was made'—Anasuya quoted in *The Story of Militant but Non-violent Trade Unionism* by MV Kamath and VB Kher

They ran the school for two hours in the morning, and two in the evening. More and more children joined, and they hired more staff. Anasuya bore all the costs of the school. She taught children the alphabet, instructed them in good values, and on the importance of cleanliness. Within two years, the children of the chawl seemed transformed!

But there was more to be done. An incident occurred that opened her eyes to the plight of the workers.

> 'I saw a group of fifteen workers passing by as if in a trance. I asked them, "What's the matter? Why do you look so listless?"
> They said, "Behen, we have just finished thirty-six straight hours of work. We have worked for two nights and a day without a break, and now we are on our way home." These words filled me with horror'—Anusuya quoted in *The Story of Militant but Non-violent Trade Unionism*

Anasuya also saw that women worked harder than men. They had to rise at 4 am to tend to their families before getting to work, and cook again, after getting back home. New mothers had to take their babies to work, and leave them asleep between the machines, breathing dusty air, full of cotton fluff.

She couldn't just sit by and watch. She started bhajan mandalis, where she also counselled workers. She became involved personally with their families, especially the women. If she heard of any instance of domestic violence, the guilty husband would be in for a tongue-lashing! She began literacy classes for the adults and also started a cooperative credit society where loans were given at reasonable rates. Now workers did not have to borrow from moneylenders at exorbitant rates.

Anasuya became a much-loved figure around the area. The workers and their families trusted her and called her Motabehn, or elder sister, a name that stayed with her for the rest of her life.

The first strike

In 1917, there was an outbreak of plague in Ahmedabad. Some of the workers fled the city and went to their villages. The mill owners were worried. What would happen to their production?

So they offered a plague bonus, a higher wage if the workers stayed back. But they did not offer this bonus to the warpers, whose job was to arrange the yarn on the beam in preparation for weaving. The reason was that most warpers were from the city itself, and didn't have a village to flee to.

The warpers decided to ask for a twenty-five per cent increase in their wages. They were earning twelve pies a day, so they would ask for fifteen pies.

They went to Anasuya for guidance. She advised the warpers to put down their demand in writing, and give the mill owners forty-eight hours to respond. If they didn't, then they would go on strike. The strike notice was sent out. It was signed by Anasuya.

Forty-eight hours passed, but there was no response from the mill owners. The warpers went on strike. The mill owners waited, thinking that the warpers would come crawling back when they found it difficult to survive. They didn't.

The mill owners tried to get substitute warpers from Bombay, but once the Bombay warpers realised why they were being called, they turned on their heels and went back, in a gesture of support for their Ahmedabad colleagues.

The strike lasted for two months. In the end, the mill owners were forced to give in. But they didn't want to look like they'd lost either. Instead of agreeing to raise the wages to fifteen pies, they announced that they'd raise it to only 14.5! Anasuya convinced the warpers to agree, and the strike was called off.

This strike was the first of its kind in India. Workers had struck work before, but most strikes were unplanned and unsuccessful, and often violent. And usually, at the end, the leaders of the strike ended up getting the sack.

There was no widespread labour movement in India before the nineteenth century. Agriculture was the prime source of employment. Even when industrialisation started, many factory workers worked only seasonally. If employment conditions were arduous, the workers just packed up and went home.

Southern India was much more active when it came to striking. There were several in the Madras Presidency: construction workers struck work in Tiruchirapally in 1859, railway workers in 1898, and there were several textile worker strikes all over south India between 1870–1891. But these strikes were seldom well organised or sustained.

On the other hand, the textile workers' strike of 1918 was well planned, had explicit aims which the workers shared with the mill owners, who were given time to respond. The strike was peaceful.

The mill owners of Ahmedabad were outraged that Anasuya, whom they considered one of their own, had organised the strike. They put pressure on Ambalal to 'discipline' his sister. In that era, Ambalal, as the head of the family, could have ordered his sister to back off. Instead, Ambalal declared that Anasuya was free to conduct her life as she wished to, and that he wasn't going to tell her what she should do!

Mahatma Gandhi had come back to India from South Africa in 1915. Though it was some time until he would become a national leader, he already was in the news, and he wielded considerable influence on the people. The Sarabhai siblings were acquainted with him, and Ambalal had donated Rs 13,000 for the running costs of the Sabarmati ashram. Gandhi had a high regard for Anasuya and her role as a labour leader, and addressed her as 'poojya', meaning worship-worthy. Anasuya also played a role in the Kheda satyagraha of 1918, and was also one of the first signatories of the Satyagraha pledge of 1919 created by Gandhi to oppose the Rowlatt Bill.

The second strike

In 1918, after the plague subsided, the mill workers heard rumours that the plague bonus would be scrapped. But life at a lower salary would be hard. The workers told Anasuya that they wanted to go on a strike for higher wages, and asked her to lead them once more.

During the warpers' strike, a few hundred people struck work. But this time, it would involve 15,000 to 20,000 people! Anasuya was uncertain how she would maintain the peace. How would she withstand the pressure from the mill owners again?

Anasuya consulted Gandhi, and with his support, decided to go ahead with the strike.

Even as the workers prepared for the strike, the mill owners decided to outsmart them and declared a lockout. They stopped production at the mills, and all 50,000 workers were thrown out, whether or not they were planning to be a part of the strike in the first place.

This was dangerous ground. There was potential for a whole lot of trouble. But Anasuya and Gandhi called for meetings, and made all the workers take a pledge that they would ask for a thirty-five per cent increase in wages, and not resume work until the demand was met, and that there would be no violence or vandalism during the strike.

Anasuya worked overtime during the lockout. She visited the workers' houses to counsel and aid. There were daily public meetings where she and other leaders updated the workers on the latest status, and the way forward. Gandhi attended some of these meetings. Anasuya issued leaflets with inspiring literature, to create a sense of calm and progress. She arranged for medical help and supplies. Her doors were always open, and she never turned people away without help or advice.

Meanwhile, the mill owners realised that their lockout strategy wasn't working. They announced that they would open the mills and welcome any workers who accepted a twenty per cent increase in wages.

In protest, Anasuya and Gandhi decided to go on a fast. 'Fasting is *my* business!!' said Gandhi, dissuading Anasuya, and went on a fast alone.

Finally after negotiations, and with the help of an arbitrator, the mill owners and the union arrived at a compromise after twenty-two days. This strike would go down in history as one of the largest strikes, conducted with peace and courtesy, and with no bitterness or violence.

Majoor Mahajan

The mill workers of Ahmedabad realised that an organised trade union would benefit them. Anasuya was asked to lead them towards this goal.

On 25 February 1920, the Majoor Mahajan was established. Nearly 40,000 out of the approximate 58,000 mill workers in the city were members. This union ensured that the workers could collectively look after their own rights (equitable wages, reasonable working hours, better quality of life) and ensure the well-being of their neighbourhoods and families.

The mill owners liked the idea of a union too. Instead of having to deal with individual complaints and grievances, they could conduct all such business through the leaders of the union.

Anasuya was made the president of Majoor Mahajan, and its first office was in her garage. She arranged for legal, social and financial experts who would provide advice and assistance.

'All the activities of our institution,' Anasuya said, 'are based on the twin principles of truth and non-violence. It is our duty to see that these principles are faithfully practised.'

Anasuya ensured a harmonious relationship between the mill owners and mill workers. She was alert to criticism of the Mahajan, and if she heard that anybody's conduct had been less than ideal, she would set things right immediately. She remained the lifetime president of the Majoor Mahajan, later renamed the Ahmedabad Textile Labour Association. It is at TLA that Ela Bhatt would become her close associate. Ela would later form the iconic Self-employed Women's Association of India.

When Anusuya died, more than 55,000 workers voluntarily contributed one day's pay towards her memorial fund. If Anasuya had known, she wouldn't have liked it at all!

WOMEN-LED LABOUR MOVEMENTS AROUND THE WORLD

Anusuya was unusual in that she was the leader of a mixed-gender trade union. While there have been many strikes led by women, these have largely been strikes by women for equal pay, such as the 1832 strike of 1,500 women card-setters in Scholes, Yorkshire, and the 1833 strike of the Women Power Loom Weavers' Association, Glasgow.

Emma Petersen [1848–1886] founded the Women's Protective and Provident League in 1874 in the UK, that became the Women's Trade Union League in 1890.

Sarah Bagley [1806–1889] was a labour leader in New England, US during the 1840s.

SOVEREIGN OF THE SILVER SCREEN

Jaddan Bai Hussain

(1892 – 8 April 1949)

> 'Directed and produced by a woman and that woman the author of the story and script, the writer of the music and songs, as well as the singer, and to crown it all, the star of the picture, *Madame Fashion*, at the Imperial Talkies, Lamington Road, has an irresistible claim upon the attention and sympathy of Bombay's film fans ... India's only woman director and producer, and one of the country's famous songstresses'—*The Times of India* (1936)

Jaddan Bai was one of the best-known musicians of her time, her admirers travelling long distances to Calcutta to hear her sing. She was also one of the first Indians to record her music on gramophone records. Then, at the height of her fame, she moved to Bombay, marched into the film industry, and made it her own. She wrote and produced her own films, directed them, composed music, sang and acted in them. And while she was at it, this remarkable woman established herself as one of the most influential figures in the Bombay film industry.

Jaddan Bai's mother Daleepa Bai was a courtesan in Allahabad. Jaddan grew up learning the arts and poetry.

By the time she was a teenager, people were remarking on her voice and talent. Daleepa Bai knew that Jaddan's talent deserved to be nurtured by the best teachers. So, they moved to Calcutta in search of the best music teachers for her.

The courtesans (tawaif) of Lucknow, Allahabad, Calcutta and Lahore were sophisticated, well-read women, who were highly accomplished in the performing arts. They contributed greatly to the development of music and dance in northern India, with mothers instructing daughters from an early age in music, dance, literature and etiquette.

Courtesans depended on the patronage of the nobility and royalty and performed in private and public gatherings at prestigious aristocratic and royal venues. Some were expert poets. Many owned land, and paid taxes, perhaps the only women in those times to do so. But because of the nature of their work, they were considered social outcasts.

While barely out of her teens, Jaddan Bai became known as an accomplished singer of Hindustani music, and a poet. She composed her own ghazals and was especially famous for her thumris. She was also extremely well-read and educated. She was charming, witty and intelligent, and could carry on a conversation about any topic.

She was soon well-established in aristocratic circles. Noblemen and rulers of princely states all over northern India, including Rampur, Bikaner, Jodhpur, Gwalior, Indore, and even far-off Kashmir, vied with each other to get Jaddan Bai to perform for them. They showered her with gold and silver, presented her with land and mansions. People flocked to listen to her.

By the time Jaddan Bai was in her late twenties, she was immensely rich, and on first-name terms with nawabs and rajas. She had two sons, Anwar Hussain and Akhtar Hussain, from her relationships with a businessman and her harmonium accompanist.

Around 1920, a medical student called Mohanchand Uttamchand fell in love with her. He asked Jaddan Bai to marry him, and she agreed. He dropped the idea of medical studies. Mohan Babu's family was aghast. Their precious, bright son was marrying a courtesan? Of a different religion? Who had two children? And he was dropping his plans to be a doctor, just to be with her? They disowned him.

Mohan Babu committed himself to helping Jaddan Bai's career. They had a daughter, whom they named Fatima.

The signs of change

Jaddan Bai knew that the courtesan tradition was on the decline. Courtesans traditionally depended on the aristocratic class and the royals for patronage and support. But these princely states were past the height of their glory. The British notions of morality made them suspicious of the courtesan tradition, and they labelled courtesans prostitutes.

Some traditional musicians refused to do recordings as they were afraid that their work would be stolen, and they felt that their music was too pure for people without the right credentials to listen to. However, many well-known courtesans, in search of new livelihoods, had no such inhibitions and went on to become radio and gramaphone artists who were highly respected and sought after, as both performers and teachers.

Sadly, they were still not always treated with respect. For example, All India Radio made a rule that their singers and artists needed to be married, as marriage was considered a sign of respectability. And even then, these artists were forced to enter the studio through a different door, so as not to come in contact with 'cultured' and 'high-born' people.

The film industry was in a fledgling state. It was a challenge to find accomplished actors. In the eyes of society in the 1930s, the industry was associated with shame and disrepute. There weren't many people, especially women, who were willing to appear on screen and risk becoming social outcasts.

And so, the time was right for Jaddan Bai and other women who had been courtesans or performing artists. They were already used to appearing before the public, and performing in front of an audience. They had no qualms about acting in movies. And they didn't really care about losing reputations because in the eyes of society, they didn't have one in the first place!

Many rapid changes were happening in the film industry. Dada Saheb Phalke made the first silent movie, *Raja Harishchandra* in 1913, but by 1931, India's first talkie, *Alam Ara*, was released and the day of the silent film was over. In *Alam Ara*, the actors talked and sang. The novelty of this attracted audiences in droves, and the film was a superhit.

The era of the talkies was calamitous for actors from the silent film era. Not many of them could sing; some didn't even know Hindi or Urdu, the languages in which most of these movies were being made.

But their loss turned out to be Jaddan Bai's gain. She had already recorded songs for the Columbia Gramophone Company, one of the first Indians to do so. She had even sung for the radio.

The break came for Jaddan Bai when the famous singer KL Saigal attended her performance. 'What a magnificent voice!' he told her. 'Your music is deeply classical, but at the same time, it has such a rustic charm!' Saigal reached out to his contacts in the film industry, and told them all about Jaddan Bai and her music.

In addition to being a renowned singer, Jaddan Bai could speak fluent Hindi, Urdu, Arabic, Bengali and Persian, and she had excellent diction. She was just what the moviemakers of Bombay and Lahore (the two centres of the Hindi and Urdu film industry) were looking for in the new era.

Hakim Ramparshad, a filmmaker of the Playart Phototone Film Company in Lahore, offered Jaddan Bai a role in the movie *Raja Gopichand*. Jaddan Bai played the mother of the male lead. Then she acted in three more movies, *Insaan ya Shaitan*, *Prem Pariksha and Seva Sadan*. The reviews were all laudatory.

The big move

Jaddan Bai observed the working of the industry, and recognised its immense potential. The next step was obvious: she would have to move to Bombay, the centre of the film industry. It was a huge step to make a complete break from an established, prosperous life in Calcutta. But she knew it had to be done.

Besides, Jaddan Bai didn't want Fatima to grow up as a courtesan. She felt that a good education and many opportunities were to be had in Bombay, and that was the way forward. She rented an apartment on Bombay's Marine Drive and moved her entire establishment there.

She reached out to patrons and contacts, and found sponsors for her venture, and tried to build a network that would help her make her way in Bombay.

Never one to do things by halves, Jaddan Bai started her own film company, Sangeet Movietone, in 1934. In 1935, she brought out her first feature film, *Talash-e-Haq*. She composed the music for this film herself, thus becoming the first woman music director in the Hindi film industry. She also wrote the story and the dialogues for the film, and she acted and sang in it.

Jaddan Bai made several movies in the next few years: *Madam Fashion* (1936), *Hriday Manthan* (1936), *Moti Ka Haar* (1937) and *Jeewan Swapna* (1937). She also acted in them.

These films served another purpose, something very important to Jaddan Bai. She used these movies as tools to alter her own image, to tell a certain story, in the way she wanted. In a way, she wrote herself into the movies. The theme of many of them was the hypocrisy of society, and about how it is possible for one to transform oneself. In her stories, the female lead starts off as not very respectable in the eyes of society, but towards the end, she gains honour and a place in society. So, through her movies, she subtly reinvented her own image. She also made it that much easier for other courtesans who were entering the film industry, ensuring that they were treated with the respect they deserved.

Jaddan Bai had the money and the contacts. But she had other assets that were priceless to her in this business. She was used to handling her own money and she had good financial sense. Besides, she was tough and smart, and she knew what she wanted. She was used to travelling alone, and didn't have to depend on anybody to go anywhere, do anything.

She also knew the art of getting things done. She knew how to speak and to whom.

Most importantly, Jaddan Bai was used to dealing with men, even (and especially) the troublesome ones. In that era, courtesans were among the few women who enjoyed friendships and conversations with men who were not family members. The ordinary interaction between the sexes that we now take for granted was a rarity back then. So Jaddan Bai was neither shy nor hesitant with men, and she knew her way around them. And inevitably, if anybody caused any problems, she knew how to deal with them, with her frank, fearless opinions, and if necessary, some pretty colourful language.

Chateau Marine

Jaddan Bai's home, in the fashionable apartment complex Chateau Marine on Marine Drive, became a meeting point for the film industry. A stream of visitors flowed in and out all day long. The kitchen was always open. Discussions on music and films filled the day. Jaddan Bai presided over soirees of music and poetry, and many informal gatherings where everybody was welcome. The who's who of Bombay's film industry were regular visitors.

She became invaluable as a source of introductions between actors and filmmakers and musicians. A recommendation from Jaddan Bai was highly valued, and many fruitful collaborations in the film industry began as a result of her introductions!

By the time her daughter Fatima was a teen, the film industry was losing its negative reputation. Actors like Devika Rani and Shobhna Samarth, who were considered 'well born', were giving it respectability. Jaddan Bai felt comfortable enough to introduce Fatima initially as a teen actor under the name of Baby Rani, and later coax her into playing the lead actor under the screen name of Nargis. Nargis was to become one of the superstars of Bollywood.

Jaddan Bai's son Anwar Hussain became an actor and her other son Akhtar Hussain a director and a film writer. His story for the movie *Raat aur Din* won Nargis a national award for best actress.

Jaddan Bai introduced several new actors, who would go on to win renown, such as Suraiya, Nimmi and, in an act that was very bold for that age, the first exotic dancer of Bollywood, Azurie. She also had a major influence on Madan Mohan, one of the greatest composers of Bollywood.

Jaddan Bai's wisdom and judgement were legendary. People approached her to solve their professional and personal problems.

> 'At times, Jaddan Bai would talk as a senior, at others as the movie producer and at times as Nargis's mother who wanted the right price paid for her daughter's work. ... Periodically, Jaddan Bai would play the conciliator'—Saadat Hasan Manto in *Stars from Another Sky*

Jaddan Bai enjoyed studying classical poetry, She also liked sports, and she liked to swim, drive, and play tennis. She owned a limousine, and enjoyed living life grandly. Some people even referred to her as Jaddan Khan, alluding to the grandness of her life and her music.

In the publicity booklet of her first movie, *Talash-e-Haq* (*Search for Truth*), Jaddan Bai writes: 'The person who lives in a dark and dismal cave has no right to complain that the sun is not shining. The sun shines only for those who step out into the sunlight. Life is full of good if we look for it.'

It's easy to believe that Jaddan Bai lived by these words.

SOME WOMEN PIONEERS IN INDIA'S FILM INDUSTRY

Ishrat Sultana (also known as Bibbo; 1906–1972) is believed to have composed music for *Adal-e-Jahangir* in 1934, a year before Jaddan Bai's film, but there are no extant recordings.

Saraswati Devi (born Khorshed Minocher-Homji; 1912–1980) was a notable music director, who composed music for Bombay Talkies Studio from 1935–41, including *Achut Kanya* (1936).

Fatma Begum (1892–1983) was the first woman film director, who made *Bulbul-e-Paristan* (1926), under the Fatma Film Company. It was a big-budget fantasy film set in fairyland.

Sulochana (born Ruby Myers; 1907–1983) was a star of silent films in the 1920s and 1930s. She was one of the highest paid actresses of her time. She started Rubi Pictures in 1939.

AROUND THE WORLD

Alice Guy-Blache (1873–1968) was a French filmmaker and producer, active largely in the US, and the first woman to make a narrative film *La Fée aux Choux (The Fairy of the Cabbages)* in 1896. In 1910, she became the first woman to run her own studio when she set up Solax. Other early US women filmmakers included **Lois Weber** and **Mabel Normand.**

Anna Hofman-Uddgren (1868–1947) was a Swedish filmmaker who made a silent film *Stockholmsfresteler* in 1911.

FIGHTING FOR FREEDOM

Lakshmi Sahgal

(24 October 1914 – 23 July 2012)

It was 4 July 1943. World War II was in full swing. Thousands of people assembled in a large field in Singapore, and the air was charged with excitement and patriotic fervour. There were soldiers from the Indian National Army (INA) in the audience, as well as civilians from the Indian immigrant community.

Singapore had been a heavily guarded British territory until 1942, when it was captured by the Japanese army. The Japanese had taken a large number of Indian soldiers in the British army prisoner. They appealed to the nationalist sentiments of the soldiers and encouraged them to become a part of the INA.

Subhash Chandra Bose stepped in front of the crowd. He had just taken over as the supreme commander of the INA.

Britain and its allies had been defeated in Malaya (the term used for the Singapore and Malaysia region) in 1941 and in Burma in 1942. The idea was that with Japanese support, the INA would fight against the British, move from Singapore to Burma, and then enter India through

Imphal. And then they would get support from the local Indians to form a greater army that could strike down the British and get independence.

In the audience was Lakshmi Swaminadhan, a twenty-eight-year-old doctor, and a member of the Indian Independence League (IIL), an organisation of expatriate Indians seeking independence. She listened agog, as Bose, his voice ringing with conviction, impressed upon the crowds that India's freedom from the British could only come through armed struggle. He stressed the need for more civilians to sign up, since the INA needed to become a large army if they had to successfully challenge the British.

'Can we put this into immediate action?' he asked.

The audience roared, and the soldiers lifted their rifles above their heads in assent.

And then Bose dropped the bombshell: 'The army will be incomplete, unless women also come forward and volunteer for the fighting ranks.'

A thrill went up Lakshmi's spine.

'For a country to be strong, its women must be educated and free,' Bose said. 'I want to raise a regiment of women, and call it the Rani of Jhansi regiment, after Rani Lakshmi Bai of Jhansi, who fought valiantly against the British in the Indian War of Independence in 1857, and died fighting.'

There were murmurs of doubt and dissent about this part of Bose's plan. But for Lakshmi, this was the highlight.

A few days later, at another rally, Bose once again stressed the importance of a women's regiment.

'I spent a sleepless night after this rally as I kept thinking of a women's regiment, wondering if it ever could be done. So far I had found little enthusiasm among Indian women for the independence movement.'—Lakshmi in *A Revolutionary Life*

The first step

Lakshmi's parents were politically active, and their children had always been encouraged to think for themselves, and voice their opinions. Lakshmi and her sister cycled, rode horses and played out of doors, unlike many other girls of the time in Madras.

Lakshmi's mother Ammu Swaminadhan was a member of the All India Women's Conference (AIWC), and Lakshmi grew up watching her mother fight for social change, justice and dignity. Though Lakshmi was fond of literature, she felt that she could serve society better as a doctor. She qualified as a gynaecologist from Madras Medical College.

Lakshmi fell in love with a pilot and married him, but within a few months, she realised marriage was not for her. She moved to Singapore with a friend, and they started a medical practice together. Her patients were mostly poor, migrant Indians who worked in plantations or did other menial jobs.

Lakshmi became an active member of the IIL. She did a radio broadcast to India in August 1942, asking people to sabotage the British war effort. After Singapore fell to the Japanese in 1942, Lakshmi plunged into relief efforts, and tended to the sick and wounded.

Inspired by Bose's speech, Lakshmi decided to drum up a women's guard of honour, and present arms to Bose at the women's rally to be held a couple of days later. She combed Singapore and found twenty women willing to get trained at short notice. That same evening, the sari-clad women assembled in a field and took instructions from two experienced INA officers. They learned the different parts of a .303 rifle, and then they were drilled for three hours on how to present arms. The next day, there followed another three hours of practice with the heavy rifles, and at the end of it, it felt like their arms would fall off.

And yet, when Bose arrived for the rally, the women stood in a row, clicked their rifles smartly, and presented arms like seasoned soldiers. It took Bose completely by surprise.

The following day, Bose asked to meet Lakshmi. The meeting lasted hours. Bose warned Lakshmi of the dangers ahead, and asked if she was prepared to take up the command of the Rani of Jhansi regiment.

Lakshmi later wrote: 'I was thrilled at the honour, but also slightly apprehensive because I knew I would have to make a complete break with my old life.' She would have to 'embrace adventure and danger'. Yet, she said, 'I had been waiting for such an involvement, so I brushed aside all my fears.' Even before Bose finished speaking, Lakshmi had offered him her unconditional support.

The following morning, Lakshmi found a car waiting to take her to the INA headquarters, where she was given an office. A tailor measured her for a uniform, and Lakshmi was good to go.

Building the regiment

Considering that this was 1942, and Lakshmi was trying to recruit women soldiers in a foreign land for the Rani of Jhansi regiment, it might have been somewhat of a challenge. But it never was.

Of the twenty women who had presented arms, fifteen volunteered. The other five declined regretfully because they had families to care for. This core group started training in a maidan near the INA headquarters. Gradually, the number of recruits rose to 100.

INA officers trained the women in the same way that the men were trained, and enforced military discipline. But they were under strict orders to instruct the women 'without corporal punishment and barracks language'.

Meanwhile, Bose went on a fund-raising mission all around southeast Asia. When he spread the word about the Rani of Jhansi regiment, young women flocked to recruiting offices, and the applications came pouring in.

Lakshmi got swamped with administration work, scrambling to find resources, and a place to house and train all these women. With Bose away, she had to approach the Japanese army herself. But they refused to cooperate. Though they were pouring in money and resources for the INA, they opposed Bose's idea of a women's regiment. Women were okay as nurses and clerks. But soldiers? However, Lakshmi persisted, and with Bose's intervention, arranged for a headquarters and a training centre for the Rani of Jhansi regiment in Singapore.

Most of the applications were from minors, who needed approval from disapproving parents to join. Since the arrangements were incomplete, eager volunteers needed reassurance that matters were on track. Over the next few months, Lakshmi travelled to Kuala Lumpur, Penang and Ipoh, reassuring parents and volunteers, talking about the INA and recruiting a large number of women.

The Ranis, as they came to be known, were from different castes, classes, religions, and social backgrounds. They spoke different languages. Yet, when they came together, all their differences fell by the wayside, and they were unified by the powerful pull of the idea of independence. It was estimated that there were in total about 1,200 women in the Rani of Jhansi regiment.

Only about one-fifth of the Ranis were educated, and some of them became commanding officers. The rest were mostly illiterate wives and daughters of Tamil labourers who worked on the rubber plantations of Malaya. Most of the Ranis were very young, just in their mid- to late teens. Some were as young as twelve. Most of them hadn't even seen India. India, for them, was just an idea, the motherland that their parents and grandparents had told them about. Yet, they identified strongly with the quest for freedom.

There were other factors, too, which made these girls join. Many of the Ranis came from poor families. They saw the army as a safe place, where they would get three square meals a day, shelter and safety from the invading Japanese army. Life in the plantations where many of them worked was hard, with conditions close to slavery. Many girls were subjected to sexual assault by plantation owners. The girls saw the army as a way out of poverty, a chance to gain self-respect. Lakshmi wrote about the girls from the plantation: 'It was the first time that somebody thought of them as individuals, individuals with value, not just as labour to make money for a boss, but a human being of use to the nation.'

For the middle-class educated women who joined, it was an opportunity to test their abilities, an adventure away from mundane domesticity, where they could use their education for a higher goal. It wasn't just the men leaving home for work, the women were leaving home too—to work for a larger cause. Lakshmi and the other commanders were role models, as women in leadership positions, and suddenly this was a possibility for all women. Moreover, the male and female recruits were paid the same salary, which was an amazing fact in itself.

Also, seeing so many women signing up for the army spurred the men into action. Many men who wouldn't have thought of joining the INA, did!

The daily schedule of the Ranis:

6.00: Hoisting the national flag

6.15–7.00: Physical training

7.30: Breakfast

8.00–10.00: Military training and squad drill

10.00–12.00: Washing and cleaning

12.00–13.30: Lunch and leisure

13.30–14.30: Classes in Romanised Hindustani

14.30–15.30: Classes in geography, the political history of India and theory of military training, strategy and tactics

15.30–17.30: Outdoor training

17.30: Roll call, lowering the national flag and singing the national anthem

19.00: Dinner, followed by conversation and music

Lakshmi's role was complex: she had to recruit women and organise camps to train them. Apart from training, she had to counsel the recruits and keep them cheerful and enthusiastic. There were training camps in Singapore, Rangoon and Bangkok.

The women received the same kind of training as their male counterparts: squad drills, training with bayonets, rifles and hand grenades, tactical exercises, climbing training. They went on route marches through hills and jungles, carrying heavy bags. And they learnt to prepare and execute schemes of attack and defence. Some were trained in jungle warfare.

> '30 March 1944 was the proudest day of my life. High-ranking INA and Japanese officers watched in astonishment as row after row of Indian women marched past and saluted as smartly as if they had been doing it all their lives. They couldn't believe that these were the same fragile, delicate and undernourished people who had responded to Netaji's call'—Lakshmi in *A Revolutionary Life*

Some 500 cadets passed out, of whom some 200 would go on to join the Chand Bibi Nursing Corps. A special point of pride for Lakshmi was that the Ranis surprised the sceptical Japanese officers with their accurate marksmanship.

The regiment marches out

About 100 Ranis marched from Malaya to Thailand, crossed the hazardous Thailand-Burma Railway, over hills and dense jungles into Burma. The plan was that they would march to the Indian border, capture Imphal, and enter India.

But a torrential monsoon storm hit the area. Marching forward would mean total destruction. The Ranis were crestfallen, but they carried on with training, nevertheless. Some Ranis volunteered for suicide squads and special service work.

But in April 1945, the regiment was asked to retreat.

As the regiment marched back despondently, they faced non-stop aerial bombardment. Their camp was bombed, and they escaped with nothing but their lives, some of them plunging into fires to save their companions. They continued tramping back through jungles, unable to even cook food for fear that smoke might give away their position to the enemy. Some were killed or injured in guerrilla ambushes. Finally, they reached Thailand, and then went back to Singapore, where the regiment was disbanded.

The British reoccupied Malaya and Burma in 1945. Intelligence officers interrogated the Ranis, expecting to find just a namesake unit, a part of what they thought was a raggedy, broken army of prisoners of war, mere puppets of the Japanese. To their astonishment, they found themselves confronted by determined young women, who proved that they were a part of an organised army fighting for a cause!

It is true that the Rani of Jhansi regiment didn't see actual fighting, were operational only for about two years, and were a small force, their numbers a fraction of the male soldiers. But the very fact that such a force was successfully established in the 1940s is astounding. Neither the US nor the UK had women in actual combat roles, though the Russian army did.

Lakshmi stayed on in the hospital camps in the jungle attending to wounded soldiers. During one march, while she was accompanying a wounded soldier to a medical centre,

Lakshmi awoke one morning to a bayonet pointed at her face. It was a group of the Japanese army who didn't know about the INA. She was tied up, until one of the soldiers happened to find a Japanese magazine with an article about the INA. Lakshmi's picture was in the newspaper, and after carefully comparing her face to the photo in the paper, he let her go.

After Independence

Lakshmi had regrets that the government did not use the foundation laid by the Ranis to build something greater after Independence.

In 1947, Lakshmi married PK Sahgal, also from the INA. She continued practising medicine. She was always involved in the social and political events of the country, such as in relief efforts during Partition, the 1971 Bangladesh War, the Bhopal gas tragedy, and the 1984 anti-Sikh riots. During the 1984 riots, she stood outside her clinic in Kanpur, chappal in hand, daring the crowds to kill any of the Sikh families in the area. The mob quietly slunk away.

She joined the CPI(M) in the 1970s and was the founder-member of All India Democratic Women's Association in 1981, which worked for social change and women's rights. She contested the presidential election against APJ Abdul Kalam. She was awarded the Padma Vibhushan.

For Lakshmi and her fellow-soldiers of the Rani of Jhansi regiment, as for countless women across the world after World War II, the war had shown that women could be out working side by side with men. This caused a profound social change. Even though many Ranis went back to where they came from, they had been transformed by their experience, and the seeds of change for women had been firmly planted.

WOMEN IN THE ARMED FORCES AROUND THE WORLD

During World War II, it was believed that men would go to war, and women would take over the other jobs—in factories, farms and offices—to keep the system running while the men were away. In the US, women were excluded from the army because it 'wouldn't be good for morale'. In Britain, trained women were sent to Europe for sabotage, assassination and spying. One of them was **Noor Inayat Khan** (1914–44), who was of Indian descent, and was posthumously decorated for her work. In many countries, women did auxiliary work in the armed forces, as nurses, drivers, telephone operators and other administrative jobs.

In World War I (1914–18) and World War II, 350 British Indian Army nurses either died or were taken prisoner of war or declared missing in action. The Women's Auxiliary Corps (India) was formed in May 1942.

In Britain and Germany, women also operated anti-aircraft guns, and searchlights, and were in charge of radar stations. In the USSR, when military reverses in 1941 led to a shortage of people enlisted in the army, Russian women worked as snipers, tank crew and bombers and pilots, and in regular combat roles. Some other European armies also had a few women soldiers.

IN INDIA

All wings of the Indian armed forces allow women in combat roles, except Indian army, where they are only allowed in support roles, and the Special Forces, where they can only be trainers. In 1992, the Indian army started inducting women officers in non-medical roles, and in April 2019, they issued the first call for women military police.

Punita Arora (b.1946) is the first Indian woman to hold the rank of lieutenant general in the India armed forces and first female vice-admiral in the Indian navy.

The Indian air force inducted three women, **Avani Chaturvedi**, **Bhawana Kanth** and **Mohana Singh**, as fighter pilots in 2016.

LIFE IN THE HOT SEAT

Indira Gandhi

(19 November 1917 – 31 October 1984)

Thirteen-year-old Indira wanted to be part of the independence movement. Her family home—Anand Bhavan in Allahabad—was itself the epicentre of the Indian freedom struggle. Her father, Jawaharlal Nehru, had been elected president of the Indian National Congress (INC) in 1929. He had drafted a resolution proclaiming that poorna swaraj, or complete independence, was the goal of the people of India. And in 1930, as the country took this pledge, Nehru called for volunteers to join the civil disobedience movement.

Indira's mother Kamala, aunts Vijayalakshmi and Krishna, and grandmother Swaroop Rani, clad in homespun cotton, addressed public meetings and went door to door to recruit more women. They all went out to picket and faced lathi charges. Kamala tended to the injured.

Nehru was imprisoned from April 1930 to January 1931. Grandfather Motilal Nehru, one of the first activists of the independence movement and a former president of the INC, was also imprisoned for his part in the civil disobedience movement, but was released when he fell ill. He was to die a few months later in 1931.

Since childhood, Indira had seen her father and grandfather get imprisoned for defying British rule. In 1921, when her father refused to pay fines to the police as a matter of principle, she had watched the police invade her home and take away property in lieu of the fine. She was used to living for long periods without members of her family, when they were away in jail or on protests.

In 1922, when her family burned their foreign-made belongings, five-year-old Indira remembered that her beloved doll was English. She was torn between love for her doll, and duty towards her country.

> 'I made my decision and, quivering with tension, I took the doll up on the roof-terrace and set fire to it. Then the tears came as if they would never stop and for some days I was ill with a temperature. To this day I hate striking a match ... [I felt] Like I was murdering someone'—Indira quoted in *Indira Gandhi* by Carol Dommermuth-Costa

When Indira played with dolls, some of her dolls represented the British, with tiny pith helmets. The Indian ones wore khadi and white Gandhi caps. The 'Indian' dolls picketed her dollhouse 'store', because it sold foreign goods. She put weapons in the hands of the 'British' dolls, but these dolls always retreated in shame. Her bedtime stories were the tales of leaders and protests. But for Indira, it wasn't enough. She wanted to be part of the real thing.

The Vanar Sena

In 1930, when her family insisted she was too young, and that she had to wait until she was eighteen to join the

INC, Indira organised the Vanar Sena, bringing together her friends, and a few other children who were eager to volunteer. The Vanar Sena was named after the army of monkeys that helped Ram look for his wife Sita in the Ramayana.

Indira took the help of leaders of the INC, and went from school to school, recruiting thousands of children. She led 15,000 of them on a procession, and even addressed crowds of 50,000 people!

The adults initially laughed at the Vanar Sena. Her grandfather wrote to her from jail, 'I would suggest that every member should wear a tail. Its length should depend on his or her office.' Indira was not amused.

The 'monkeys' took over the routine chores of the INC, and acted as messengers. They prepared food and drink for protesters, distributed pamphlets, sewed and hoisted flags, tended to wounded protesters, addressed envelopes, wrote letters for jailed freedom fighters and collected rations for volunteer camps. As the general of the army, Indira instructed her volunteers to collect one paisa from every household for the Vanar Sena Paisa Fund.

They also gathered intelligence. They hung around police stations, and found out when the next raid or arrest would take place. Since people habitually underestimate children, no one thought to pay attention to the odd lurking child.

Indira even smuggled a document about a revolutionary plan out of her home, in her school bag, because the elders were under police surveillance. When the police stopped Indira, she declared that she was already late for school and escaped.

> 'She is—and I am glad of it—a high-spirited girl. I would rather have an ounce of spirit in her than a pound of learning. But learning and mind-training is also necessary and so I do hope that she will pay attention to those'—Nehru, quoted in *Indira Gandhi* by Pupul Jayakar

Indira had studied in multiple schools. When Kamala travelled to Geneva, Switzerland, for treatment for tuberculosis, Indira enrolled in L'Ecole International there in 1926. She explored Geneva, interacted with classmates of varying nationalities and visited neighbouring countries. The school also taught gymnastics, dancing and gardening. Besides, on their walks to and from school, she had the opportunity to converse deeply with her father.

In 1927, she joined St Mary's Convent, Allahabad, and in 1931, People's Own School, Poona, a boarding school. As the oldest student, Indira had to look after the younger ones, washing and feeding them. Her father in jail and her mother sick, Indira often cried herself to sleep, but she stuck it out. She often visited Mahatma Gandhi at the Poona prison and grew close to him. After leaving school, she studied in Tagore's Shantiniketan.

Her mother died when Indira was eighteen. She had always been a lonely child, and the loss of her mother made it worse. She carried the grief well into her adulthood.

In 1936, she joined Somerville College, Oxford, where she studied history, anthropology and administration. The start of World War II forced her to come back to India without completing her degree.

But the most important part of her education was not at any of these schools. She grew up in an environment in which national and international politics was discussed all the time. Nehru regularly wrote letters to her from jail, talking to her about history, civilisation, society and natural history. These letters were published much later as *Letters from a Father to His Daughter*.

The road to Independence

Indira was a reluctant public speaker. In 1937, VK Krishna Menon, politician, diplomat and Nehru's friend, invited her to speak at a gathering of social activists in Caxton Hall, London. Her fame preceded her, and Indira was terrified, especially because the hall was so big. As she spoke, a drunken man called out, 'She doesn't speak, she squeaks!' The hall erupted with laughter.

'I will never, never speak in public again,' Indira declared to herself.

On the way from London to India, Indira stopped at Cape Town, South Africa. She was invited to speak at a reception, but though she agreed to attend, she declined to speak. However, before the event, she visited an area where black railway workers lived, and their terrible living conditions overwhelmed her. When she reached the event, she declared that she did wish to speak, and held forth to the largely white audience about how necessary it was for them to work together with black people.

When Indira was studying in Oxford, she joined the student wing of the British Labour Party. She organised fund-raisers for medical aid in China, and auctioned her jewellery for money for the Spanish Civil War, and boycotted Japanese goods when Japan attacked China in

1937. When there were Germans air raids on London in 1940, she joined the Red Cross as a volunteer, drove an ambulance and tended to victims of air raids.

In 1942, Indira married Feroze Gandhi, a journalist and a fellow activist in the freedom struggle. The couple participated in the Quit India movement of 1942, and were jailed. 'No one who has not been in prison for any length of time can ever visualise the numbness of sprit that can creep over one,' she wrote later. Being released 'was like coming suddenly out of a dark passage. I was dazzled with the rush of life, the many hues and textures, the scale of sounds and the range of ideas. Just to touch and listen was a disturbing experience and it took a while to get adjusted to normal living.'

During the Partition of India, in 1947, millions of refugees crossed the border on either side. Violence often broke out between Hindus and Muslims. Indira went to refugee camps to provide relief and help maintain peace. She travelled to particularly troubled areas, arranged for food and medical supplies, and helped with sanitary and other problems.

On one such instance, Indira saw a man being chased by hundreds of people. Without thinking, she jumped out of her car and ran barefoot to the man and pushed him behind her. He clung to her sari, terrified, as she turned around and faced the crowd.

'You can only kill this man after you have killed me!' she said. The crowd hadn't recognised her, and they said they would kill her.

'You don't have the courage, and you will not!' she said, and finally the crowd let both Indira and the man go.

The road to the top

Indira had joined the INC in 1938. She became a member of the Congress Working Committee in 1955. In 1959, she became the president of the INC. 'The higher one climbs,' she said, 'the more hazardous the journey and the narrower and steeper the trail.'

During Nehru's tenure as prime minister (1947–64), Indira served as a hostess for her father, welcoming diplomats and world leaders at his home and accompanying him on his official trips abroad. She also travelled on her own, as Nehru's representative, as he got older. Indira had always been reticent and quiet, and so, she didn't particularly enjoy all this social interaction. She later said, 'It took me a long time to get over this. But I had to learn to enjoy it, so I did.' As Nehru grew older, he came to rely on her more and more. The stress took a toll on her health and she fell sick often.

It also affected her married life. As Indira's responsibilities towards her father increased, she spent more and more time away from Feroze. In today's world, it is common for couples to stay apart for work, but in the 1950s and 1960s, it was highly unusual, and both Feroze and the society at large didn't take it well. Indira was also unhappy that she couldn't spend as much time as she wanted to with her two young sons. As one of the first women in Indian politics to juggle both work and family, the hurdles and social disapproval must have lain heavily on her shoulders.

In 1964, Indira became a Rajya Sabha member. Prime Minister Lal Bahadur Shastri made her the minister of information and broadcasting in his government from 1964 to 1966. When Shastri died in office in 1966, the INC held an election to select its leader.

In spite of her experience and the fact that she showed political promise, INC leaders didn't think too highly of Indira. They saw her as a weak, powerless woman, and called her 'goongi gudiya' (mute doll) behind her back. Some leaders thought that if they could persuade her to stand against veteran Morarji Desai and win the party leadership, they could manipulate her and take control of the party.

Indira defeated Morarji Desai in this election, and became the third prime minister of India on 24 January 1966. But later, the joke turned out to be on those leaders who underestimated her. Indira took control of her own affairs, and when general elections were held the following year, Indira came to power again. She was prime minister for three consecutive terms, from 1966 to 1977, and then a fourth term, from 1980 till she was assassinated in 1984.

The road to glory

> 'Probably no woman in history has assumed a heavier burden of responsibility and certainly no country of India's importance has ever before entrusted so much power to a woman'—*The Guardian* (1966)

What established Indira's reputation as a decisive leader, and silenced all critics of a women head of government was her decisive military intervention in the formation of Bangladesh.

In 1970, Mujibur Rahman, the elected leader of East Pakistan, was arrested on the orders of General Yahya Khan of Pakistan. Rahman's followers rose up and declared independence. The Pakistan army conducted air strikes and military operations in East Pakistan in 1971, and millions of refugees fled to India. India sent forces to aid East Pakistan, and achieved a quick and stunning victory in thirteen days. In 1972, Rahman became the first prime minister of the new country of Bangladesh.

With this victory, India's position as a dominant power in south Asia was underlined, and Indira was called a brilliant military strategist and diplomat. Those who had doubted that a woman could take hard military decisions were silenced. *The Economist* referred to her as 'Empress of India', and even opposition leaders compared her to the Hindu goddess Durga.

Her first terms also saw significant economic consolidation. Indira took over as prime minister at a time when the exuberance of being newly independent had passed, and there was need for hard-core development work. Some of her significant undertakings includes the nationalisation of banks (1969, 1980), the continuation of the Green Revolution, the White Revolution (1970), abolition of the privy purses (1971), the detonation of the Smiling Buddha (1974) and the launch of the first unmanned satellite *Aryabhatta* (1975).

In spite of her proving herself a tough, strong-willed and decisive leader, Indira faced obstacles that a man in her place would perhaps not have. In her initial years in politics, she had to consciously move out of Nehru's shadow. In her words, 'one has to work doubly hard to show one is not merely a daughter but is also a person in her own right. Of course, being a woman you have to work twice as hard as a man.'

She received death threats and insults all through her career. Apart from 'goongi gudiya', she was also called a schoolgirl and a 'chhokri' (girl) by her opponents, and US president Nixon refered to her as 'an old witch'.

Asked to describe herself, Indira once told a journalist, 'In spite of always living in the public glare, she has remained a very private person. Her life has been hard. This has made her self-reliant but has not hardened her.'

The dark years

Though Indira's faction of the INC, Congress (R), had come to power in 1971 with a huge majority on the slogan 'Garibi Hatao' (abolish poverty), there hadn't been much change in the state of poverty, starvation and debt in which millions lived. There were strikes and protests, and Indira's political opponents spoke out against what they called her inefficiency and corruption. In 1975, Indira was found guilty of election malpractice, and banned from holding elected office for six years.

When her opponents called for her to resign, Indira declared emergency rule in the country on 25 June 1975, which gave her virtually unlimited power.

The Emergency resulted in violations of civil rights. Thousands of protestors, activists and political opponents, were imprisoned and tortured. The media was muzzled; the courts made powerless. There were numerous atrocities committed against civilians. A birth-control programme led by Indira's son Sanjay sterilised people against their will.

Emergency was withdrawn on 21 March 1977, and the next general elections were the same year. The Congress (R) was resoundingly defeated, and the Janata party came to power. But the Janata party was divided, and so, Congress (R) came back to power in the next general elections, and Indira became prime minister again in January 1980.

In the early 1980s, some members of the Sikh community started calling for a separate nation, Khalistan. Violence spread, and some extremists, led by militant religious leader, Jarnail Singh Bhindranwale, took control of the Golden Temple in Amritsar, which was turned into an armoury. In June 1984, Indira gave the army the go-ahead for Operation Bluestar, and the army moved their tanks and troops into the Golden Temple. It resulted in tremendous loss of life, not just of Bhindranwale and his supporters, but of soldiers and innocent people. Sikhs the world over were devastated at the desecration of their holy place.

Shortly afterwards, Indira's Sikh bodyguards assassinated her on 31 October 1984, in retaliation for Operation Bluestar. Following her death, thousands of Sikhs were killed and millions displaced in the anti-Sikh riots, one of the most shameful incidents in the post-Independence history of India.

SOME PIONEER WOMEN POLITICIANS IN INDEPENDENT INDIA

Amrit Kaur (1889–1964) was the health minister of India in the union cabinet 1947–57.

Sucheta Kripalani (1908–74) was first woman chief minister, of Uttar Pradesh 1963–67.

Sarojini Naidu (1879–1949) was the first woman governor of an Indian state (Uttar Pradesh) from 1947–49.

AROUND THE WORLD

Sirimavo Bandaranaike (1916–2000) became the world's first non-hereditary female head of government in modern history when she became prime minister of Sri Lanka in 1960.

WOMEN IN TECH

A Lalitha

(27 August 1919 – 12 October 1981)

What's common between computer compilers, caller ID, windscreen wipers, space station batteries, dishwashers, disposable diapers, home security systems, solar-heated homes, foot-pedal dustbins, bulletproof vests and invisible glass? (Apart from being part of a futuristic novel about a hygienically-inclined baby spy?)

They were all invented by women.

The field of engineering studies was considered strictly a male domain for a long time. In India, the barrier breakers were three women, A Lalitha, PK Thressia and Leelamma George. They graduated in 1943 from College of Engineering, Guindy (CEG), India's oldest tech institution (founded in 1794).

> 'Old barriers are breaking down and the world is on the brink of diving into a new order. Can half the population of the world afford to be ignorant of a science and profession responsible for the creation and maintenance of the present-day civilisation?'— Lalitha and Leelamma in an essay 'Eves in Engineering' in *Survey School to Tech Temple* (1941)

A Lalitha was the first woman electrical engineer in India. She got married when she was just fifteen, completed her tenth standard soon after, and then left school. Lalitha had a baby at eighteen, but when little Syamala was just four months old, her father died.

Lalitha had to find a way to support herself and her child. She decided to go to college, and get a professional degree. But what would she study?

Lalitha's father was a professor of electrical engineering at CEG. In fact, Lalitha's family was full of engineers, and she herself was inclined towards the subject. However, no woman had ever studied engineering in India. Would colleges even admit women?

Lalitha's father spoke to the principal of CEG about his daughter's wish. The principal was farsighted enough to realise that it was time women entered the field. Permission was obtained from the Director of Public Instruction in the British government, and in 1939, A Lalitha joined the electrical engineering department of CEG.

It wasn't easy for Lalitha to be the only woman at a time when men and women who were unrelated didn't speak to each other. There was nobody in college to talk to, or discuss studies with.

Lalitha's father placed an ad in the newspapers, calling for more women to join the engineering course at CEG. Two women responded: PK Thressia and Leelamma George, both of whom joined the civil engineering course. There were no hostel facilities for women on campus, but they found accommodation off campus. Life became easier now that there were three of them.

The three women graduated in 1943. The pre-printed degree certificates said 'he', so that had to be struck out and 'she' hand-written. Lalitha stayed on for one more year and completed her honours degree from the same college, and then did a year's apprenticeship in Jamalpur Railway Workshop.

Work struggles

It wasn't hard to find a job. But Lalitha was forced to be choosy about where she would work. As a single mother, living alone with her daughter in a strange city wouldn't have been easy in the 1940s. She joined Central Standards Organisation of India (CSOI) as an engineering assistant. The job was at Shimla, where her brother's family lived, and she lived with them.

After she'd worked there for a bit, Lalitha was promoted, but some of her colleagues (male, obviously) didn't approve, so they cancelled her promotion.

In 1946, Lalitha's father asked her to help with his research on electrical devices. She joined him, and they did some fruitful work together—he patented a Jelectromonium (an electrical musical instrument), smokeless ovens and an electric flame producer. However, by 1948, Lalitha realised she had to get back to a regular job as she needed the money.

Lalitha joined the Calcutta office of Associated Electrical Industries (AEI), a UK-based company, later taken over by General Electric. Another of Lalitha's brothers lived in that city, so Lalitha and her daughter lived with his family for many years.

Lalitha was a design engineer in AEI and worked on transmission lines, and to solve problems related to substations and protective gear. She also dealt with contracts. She spent more than thirty years at AEI and enjoyed her job, but she couldn't reach her full potential professionally. Her male colleagues were sent out to work on location at installation sites, but her bosses used Lalitha's single-mother status as a reason to not send her on-site. However, a few years later, she was thrilled to get an opportunity to work on the electrical generators of the Bhakra Nangal Dam, one of the earliest and largest of India's hydroelectric power projects in Himachal Pradesh.

Lalitha became a member of the Institution of Electrical Engineers, London. In 1964, the Society of Women Engineers in the US organised the first International Conference of Women Engineers and Scientists (ICWES) in New York. The goal of the conference was to encourage more women to participate in science, technology, engineering and mathematics. They invited Lalitha to speak; she was the only representative from India.

Lalitha became a member of the Women's Engineering Society (WES) of London in 1965. The WES volunteered to host the second ICWES in Cambridge UK. Lalitha worked hard to publicise the event, and enabled five women engineers from India to attend this conference.

Lalitha had a long and successful career. She retired in 1977, and died two years later.

SOME PIONEER INDIAN WOMEN ENGINEERS

Lalitha's two college mates also stormed new domains.

PK Thressia (1924–1981) became India's (and perhaps Asia's) first woman chief engineer of a state public works department when she headed the Kozhikode Roads and Buildings department in 1971.

Leelamma George (1923–1989) joined the public works department of Travancore, studied town planning in the UK and eastern Europe, and retired as the assistant chief engineer in 1978.

Rajeshwari Chatterjee (1922–2010) had a master's degree in engineering and a PhD in 1953 from the US. She was IISc's first female faculty, when she became professor of engineering, and later headed the electrical communication department.

AROUND THE WORLD

Many of the women who did pioneering engineering work did not have academic degrees.

Margaret Hamilton (b.1936) from US is best known for writing the code that helped send humans to the moon. She also coined the term 'software engineering'.

Ada Lovelace (1815–1852) from UK wrote the first computer programme for Charles Babbage's digital computer in the 1840s.

Emily Roebling (1843–1903) was the wife of the chief engineer of the Brooklyn Bridge, New York, but when he fell ill, she took over as the chief engineer with all its managerial and technical responsibilities, and completed the bridge.

Ellen Henrietta Swallow Richards (1842–1911) was the first woman in the US to study engineering, in MIT. She graduated in 1873, but wasn't awarded a degree. She went on to work as an industrial and safety engineer, environmental chemist, and university faculty member.

Elizabeth Bragg (1854–1929) was the first US woman to get an engineering degree, in civil engineering in 1876 from the University of California, Berkeley. She never worked as an engineer, though.

Julia Morgan (1872–1957) graduated from UC, Berkeley in 1894, and became an architect who designed more than 700 buildings in California.

Alice Perry (1885–1969) was the first woman to get an engineering degree in Europe, from Queen's College, Galways in 1906. She subsequently worked as a county surveyor and was a women's rights activist and poet.

Mary Kies (1752–1857) was the first woman to receive a US patent was in 1809, for her method of weaving straw with silk.

Hertha Ayrton (1854–1923) was a British engineer, mathematician, physicist and inventor. She became the first woman member of the Institution of Electrical Engineers in 1899, and the first woman nominated to be a Fellow of the Royal Society of London in 1902.

Sarah Guppy (1770–1852) was the first British woman to receive a patent in 1811 for a method of making safe piling for bridges. She went on to design and patent a range of products.

THE DETERMINED DIPLOMAT

CB Muthamma

(24 January 1924 – 14 October 2009)

'This is not the right field for a woman.'

The setting was an interview room in New Delhi in 1948. The all-male interview panel of the Union Public Service Commission (UPSC) was headed by the chairman of the UPSC, who spoke these words. The interviewee was CB Muthamma.

Muthamma had comfortably topped the civil services written examination. She had indicated in her application that she wanted to join the Indian Foreign Service (IFS). And now, at the interview, the panel took one look at her and was suddenly seized with doubts about her abilities.

> 'As long as I was an anonymous number in a question paper, I had been consistently at the top. But when the anonymous number materialised as a woman, the response was different!'— Muthamma in *Slain by the System: India's Real Crisis*

Until 1854, India's administrators were appointed by the East India Company directors. Then merit-based Indian Civil Service was introduced, with examinations held at London.

Only a handful of Indians were able to attend and qualify (Satyendranath Tagore, brother of Rabindranath Tagore, was the first, in 1863). From 1922, the Indian Civil Service Examination began to be held in India as well as London, and more Indians were able to qualify. The modern civil services was formed after 1947. Examinations are conducted nationwide to recruit candidates for the different branches of the civil services.

In many ways, the newly-independent India was ahead of other countries in recognising the equality of men and women. The Constitution, which would come into effect in 1950, specified that there should be no discrimination anywhere, on the basis of sex. The principle was already in effect, and the examinations for the civil services had been made open to both men and women.

Muthamma was backed by a fiercely independent mother, who believed that her children could do anything. And she was inspired by Mahatma Gandhi, who had asked women to come out of their domestic seclusion and take part in the affairs of the country.

Muthamma's father was a forest officer, but he died when she was nine years old. Her mother had known what it felt like to have doors closed on her because she was a girl. Even with her limited resources, she gave her four children an education in the best schools and colleges within her reach.

And Muthamma did her credit. After studying in St Joseph's Girls School in Madikeri, Karnataka, she went to Madras and graduated from Women's Christian College with three gold medals. She did her post-graduation in English literature from Presidency College, Madras before sitting for the civil service examinations.

> 'Having a supportive mother and an enlightened Constitution was one thing. But what was I to do against the traditional bias of men against women?'—Muthamma in *Slain by the System: India's Real Crisis*

At the interview, Muthamma did the only thing she could: she stood her ground and insisted that she would join the IFS. The chairman of the UPSC did the only thing *he* could–he used his influence to make sure that Muthamma was awarded the minimum possible marks in the interview, hoping that this would disqualify her. (Many years later, after he retired, he told Muthamma that he had done this.)

But Muthamma's performance in the written exams had been so good, that in spite of her abysmal marks in the interview, she stood third in the IFS list. In 1949, Muthamma became the first woman to join the IFS.

Other women weren't so fortunate. One woman, who made it to the interview, met an unsympathetic medical examination board. They found nothing wrong with her health, so they disqualified her by stating that she wasn't the right weight for her height.

Anti-woman bias

> 'Looking back, I cannot help but conclude that my entire tenure with the External Affairs Ministry was one long tussle with the anti-woman bias. Being the only woman in the service in its formative stage, I was the first one to run into every hurdle'—Muthamma in *Slain by the System: India's Real Crisis*

The ministry of external affairs (MEA), under which the IFS comes, initially found it hard to give Muthamma any postings abroad. All the Indian diplomatic missions and the offices of the ambassadors resisted her joining, and individually came up with the same perplexing justification: 'She might have to go to the airport in the middle of the night.'

But finally, the MEA posted Muthamma as third secretary at the embassy at Paris.

Muthamma's bosses at the embassy made things difficult for her, and tried hard to prove that they were right in resisting having her there. But when the political counsellor had to step away from office for a while, Muthamma took over. By the time he got back to work, everybody had to admit that Muthamma had done a good job. After that, things got better for her.

But at every new posting, the pattern repeated.

When Muthamma joined, she was made to sign an agreement that she would resign if she got married. Male candidates had no such conditions. It didn't occur to her to challenge this rule. Muthamma did not marry, but some female colleagues were forced to resign when they did. The 'logic', allegedly, was that if female officers got married, they might leak national secrets to their husbands!

In 1961, two officers, Manorama Kocchar and Hardev Bhalla, decided to get married. The then-prime minister Jawaharlal Nehru was known to want to see more women in the diplomatic field. Kocchar wrote to Nehru, and received permission to marry, and for Kocchar to continue working in the IFS.

Head of mission

In 1970, Muthamma became the first Indian woman career diplomat to be appointed ambassador. She was posted as the head of mission to Hungary.

The rulebook said that an ambassador who was single could take along a close female relative to help run their household. Muthamma asked for permission to take her mother as her hostess. But the head of the administration in the ministry was convinced that this rule was only for male ambassadors, because the rulebook said 'he', not 'she'. And he wouldn't budge from his interpretation. Muthamma thought of taking legal action against the ministry for discrimination against women. Finally, wrote Muthamma, 'it was only after persistent, devious and utterly inane battles that official clearance was given to me, thus allowing women thereafter to benefit from this particular rule.'

Her posting had unexpected repercussions. Until then, Hungary had refused to send women as ambassadors to its diplomatic missions, though there were highly capable women in the ranks. But now India was asking to send a woman ambassador to Hungary. Hungary was a communist country and they were eager to make friends with non-aligned nations like India. So, they couldn't refuse India's request. Besides, communist countries proclaimed that they were in favour of equality of the sexes. So they accepted India's request.

Women's organisations in Hungary demanded that they needed better opportunities too. So, it was during Muthamma's posting at Hungary that Hungary sent out its first woman ambassador!

Taking on the government

In 1979, Muthamma noticed that it was taking very long for her to be promoted to the highest level in the IFS, and her male juniors being promoted over her. She had good reason to suspect that she, and another female colleague, were being passed over because they were women.

When she asked why they weren't being promoted to the secretary-level grade, she was told it was on grounds of 'merit'. When she received the foreign secretary's letter informing her of this decision, she wrote back to say that while she completely agreed that promotion should be on merit, she wanted to know how they assessed her merit. No response.

She wrote to the minister of external affairs. Still no response.

Muthamma had seen enough discrimination. She decided that the system needed to change. She took a step that would make history: she took the government of India to court. Her other woman colleague refused to join her for fear of repercussions.

In her petition to the Supreme Court in 1979, Muthamma said that she had been denied promotion because she was a woman and that there was a long-standing practice of hostile discrimination against women in the service. She also challenged the rules governing the employment of women that are discriminatory in nature. For instance, she had been required to sign an agreement that she would resign if she got married. Married women weren't appointed to the IFS at all; if a woman officer did get permission to marry, the government could still remove her from her position if they thought that her marriage had been preventing her from doing her work properly. These rules contradicted two articles in the Constitution: Article 12, which guarantees equality before the law, and Article 16, which protects equality of opportunity in matters of public employment.

Immediately after the case went to court, Muthamma was promoted to secretary level. The ministry probably hoped Muthamma would drop the case. But she didn't.

The three-member bench in the Supreme Court was headed by Justice VR Krishna Iyer. The bench examined the case, and said that it was difficult to believe that such rules and discrimination existed thirty years after Independence. The rules were clearly unconstitutional. If family and domestic commitments came in the way of working efficiently, it should be true for both men and women. If there is a danger of leakage of national secrets due to being married, it should hold good for both men and women. The court recommended that the government overhaul all service rules to remove gender discrimination.

The Supreme Court verdict in the CB Muthamma vs Union of India was a landmark judgement and a huge step for gender equality in India.

Women in different fields were inspired to file similar cases challenging gender discrimination. For example, the air hostesses of Air India went to court against gender discrimination related to marriage, pregnancy and the retirement age.

Over the years, a number of women had become IFS officers. But though there were now more women in the workplace, the prejudice didn't go away. Many people believed that women had only one role in the world of diplomacy—to be good hostesses! Female officers were seen as odd, to be reluctantly tolerated. To cap it, women were paid less for the same position than men.

Shortly after the Supreme Court judgement, women IFS officers received letters from the MEA, saying that if they wanted to continue in service, they shouldn't ask to be posted to the same place as their husbands. The fact was that men also often asked to be posted to the same place as their wives, but the men didn't get similar letters. When the women officers got together to protest against the discriminatory letter, male colleagues offered to speak on their behalf. 'We are perfectly capable of representing our own case,' said the women, and threatened to go to court. The ministry quietly withdrew the letter.

The struggle continues

After Paris, Muthamma was posted to Rangoon and London. Later, she was posted to the important division dealing with Pakistan in New Delhi. She followed this by heading another sought-after division, the Americas. After her first posting as ambassador to Hungary in Budapest, she was posted as ambassador to Ghana in Accra, and her last posting was to the Netherlands in the Hague.

Former foreign secretary Chokila Iyer wrote about Muthamma's posting in Accra, 'The stories that she used to recount of the impossible conditions those days! Thank god our valiant diplomat hung tough; any lesser personage would have thrown in the sponge.'

'Greater attention will have to be given to affect generational changes by ensuring the correct conditioning of children's minds before they settle into the rut of traditionalist thinking'— Muthamma in *Slain by the System: India's Real Crisis*

Muthamma won the Carnegie Fellowship for Policy Planning and the fellowship of the Indian Institute of Advanced Studies. After she retired, she was a member of the Palme Commission, a non-governmental commission on disarmament and security issues set up by Swedish prime minister Olof Palme.

Muthamma was involved in helping riot victims after the anti-Sikh riots of 1984 and the Babri Masjid demolition of 1993. She worked for various causes she believed in: electoral fair practices and the environment. She donated land for an orphanage started by Missionaries of Charity, and just a week before her death, she donated money for a school library and a business management college in Kodagu.

Muthamma wrote numerous articles on the challenges that India faces, about foreign affairs, constitutional reforms, education, culture and women, many of which were compiled into a book: *Slain by the System: India's Real Crisis*. She also co-authored a cookbook of forgotten Kodava recipes.

SOME OF INDIA'S WOMEN DIPLOMATS

Vijaya Lakshmi Pandit (1900–1990) was the first Indian female ambassador, to the USSR in 1947, and later to other countries. This was a political appointment. She was also elected as the first female president of the United Nations General Assembly (1953–54).

Chokila Iyer (b.1943) became India's first woman foreign secretary, or the administrative head of the MEA, in 2001.

AROUND THE WORLD

Rosika Bédy-Schwimmer (1877–1948) was a pacifist, feminist and suffragist, who served as the Hungarian ambassador to Switzerland in 1918.

Diana Apcar (1859–1937) was posted as Armenian ambassador to Japan in 1920. But this was a political appointment.

Chile also had several female ambassadors in the 1930s, such as **Olga de la Barra**, **Ines Ortuzar** and **Gabriela Mistral**.

Lucile Atcherson (1894–1986) was the first woman in foreign service in the world, who joined the US foreign service in 1922.

Suzanne Borel (1904–1994) of France joined her country's foreign service in 1930.

Frances Elizabeth Willis (1899–1983) was the first US woman career diplomat to be appointed ambassador, when she became the ambassador to Switzerland in 1953.

GOING FOR GOLD

PT Usha

(b. 27 June 1964)

Pilavullakandi Thekkeparampil Usha reigned over the world of track and field for over two decades. She is perhaps the most-talked-about Indian athlete, even now, though it's been nearly twenty years since she retired.

Usha was the first Indian woman to reach an Olympic final event. She was also the youngest Indian to qualify for the Olympics.

Usha won 101 medals in international track and field events, a number that no other Indian athlete has even come close to matching. Her five-gold-medal haul in the 1985 Jakarta Asian Championships is the world record for the most gold medals won by an individual at a single athletic event. It is also the only world record of any kind held by an Indian in track and field.

Between 1982 and 1998, she was by far the fastest runner in Asia. She won four gold and six silvers in four Asian Games, and twenty-two medals (fourteen gold) in the Asian Athletic Championships.

When she retired at the age of thirty-six, she was ranked the best athlete in India! No wonder her nicknames include

Payyoli Express, Udan Pari, Golden Girl, and Queen of Indian Track and Field.

As fast as she could

When Usha was little, she kept falling sick. Not a very promising beginning for somebody who would come to be known for speed. But she loved to jump over fences (when she was not sick, we hope). Her father, EPM Paithal, was a cloth merchant, and her mother, Lakshmi, was a school teacher. They didn't have much money, and six children to look after. So they had other things to worry about, and didn't particularly notice that Usha seemed to be a pretty fast runner.

But her physical education teacher at school noticed. One day, when she was eight, her teacher told her to race a twelve-year-old from the same school, who was the district champion.

'I had never run a race before,' said Usha. 'But I was excited to run against this chechi (older sister). All I wanted to do was win, so I ran as fast as I could!'

And she won! She couldn't believe that she had outrun the champion. Neither could the spectators. Her teachers encouraged her to participate in interschool competitions. But her parents weren't so sure.

'Inititally, my dad did not want me to take up sports; he was worried that I would get injured,' said Usha. 'I was good in science in school and my parents thought I would become a school teacher like my mother.'

When they saw how good Usha was, they were impressed. But they had no idea how to guide her. Forget taking up sports as a career, racing itself wasn't common among girls.

By 1976, Usha started winning the sub-zilla races. And yet, when she studied about the Olympics at school in seventh standard, it seemed to be a vague, far-off idea. 'I didn't imagine that I would participate in the Olympics some day!' she said.

The following year, the Kerala government started a sports school for women. Usha applied and was selected. She stayed in the hostel and trained rigorously every day. She participated in as many tournaments as she could, and won almost every event. She invariably bagged the championship trophy.

The other important event in her life was that she met OM Nambiar, who recognised that Usha had what was needed to win big. 'He coaxed us to do more exercises by offering us sweets,' said Usha. 'I used to get a lot of them!'

Nambiar would later become her personal coach, and their partnership lasted for twenty-six years. The Indian government even gave OM Nambiar the Dronacharya award, given to coaches, for his role in Usha's achievements.

Usha's first international event was the 1980 Pakistan Open National Meet in Karachi. She had travelled by train, with no reservation. Random passers-by threw dung bombs at the train and one of them hit her on the face. But she collected four gold medals in Karachi and became famous throughout India.

The first Olympics

In the same year, she qualified for the 100m of the 1980 Moscow Olympics. At sixteen, she was the youngest Indian ever to qualify for the Olympics.

Her journey to Moscow (in the erstwhile USSR) was her first flight ever. And it didn't agree with her at all. She had a terrible headache by the time she reached the Olympic village. She was tired and thirsty and downed the first welcome drink she found. She still doesn't know what it was (wine, she wonders) but it made her headache worse. She kept throwing up the first day.

The rest of the Indian contingent was senior to her and all the buildings in the Olympic village looked similar to her. She kept losing her way to and from her room, and often arrived at the mess late, to find all the containers of Indian food empty! But in spite of all this, the excitement of being at the Olympic tracks was immense.

'It was a thrill just standing on the tracks!' she said. But that thrill quickly dissolved as she looked around at her fellow athletes. 'They were strong and muscular,' said Usha. 'My entire body was as big as a single leg of theirs!'

She was pretty sure she wouldn't win—she was a total newbie without any training, and these athletes were much better and more experienced than her.

But 'I didn't want to finish last!' she said. 'I cannot even imagine coming in last!' She ran in the heats, and didn't qualify for the semi-finals. But she did manage to come in sixth.

The first Olympic finals

By the time the next Olympics came around, in 1984 in Los Angeles, Usha was twenty, a seasoned athlete, with more international meets and medals (and more flights) to her credit. But her coach got her to change her main event to the 400m hurdles. This was not an event for which she had any international exposure, and she didn't have a training partner with whom she could practice, a crucial part of any prep. But Nambiar entered her name into the pre-Olympics trials anyway. She beat the top US runner Judi Brown in this event, and it gave her a burst of confidence.

At the Games, she clocked 56.81 seconds in the heats and 55.54 seconds in the semi-final, which was a new Commonwealth record.

It was with this confidence that she went into the final Olympic race. She had planned her strategy and her strides between each hurdle. She would start off quickly, relax her pace in the middle, and then give it her all in the final sprint.

It went according to plan at first. She got off to a great start, one of the most essential parts of winning a race. But one of the other athletes had a false start, and so the race was recalled.

This was where Usha's inexperience raised its head. 'I lost focus,' she said. 'I was extremely nervous and tense. My arms were shivering.'

But there was nothing else to do; she had to give it another go. This time, she didn't get a good start. Mid-race, she had to rethink her strategy. She surged forward, and caught up with the rest of the runners. At one point, she was running in second place, matching the others stride by stride, leap by leap.

In the final stretch, her strength gave out as the runners behind her caught up with her. It was a photo finish, with three runners crossing the line at almost the same time.

When the results came in, she found that her time was 55.42 seconds, an Asian best. (It still stands as India's national record.) But the bronze-winning time was 55.41 seconds. She had lost out on an Olympic medal by .01 second.

Try and wrap your head around what a teeny, tiny, titchy period of time that is. She was completely shattered. 'I had the medal in my hands, and I let it go,' she said.

The champion of Asia

Usha's mastery over the tracks made itself obvious in the world of Asian athletics. For years, she was the undisputed champion of the continent.

Even though she had missed the medal at Los Angeles, she was quite aware of what a splendid performance she had given. Besides, she got the opportunity to train in London for a few months, for the 1985 Asian Athletics Championships at Jakarta. She won five gold medals there, including the coveted 100m sprint, establishing herself as the fastest woman in Asia. No other male or female athlete anywhere in the world has won so many golds at a single international athletic event ever!

At the 1986 Asian Games at Seoul, she won four golds in the 200m, 400m, 400m hurdles and 4x400m relay. She had to settle for a silver in the 100m, losing out to Lydia de Vega of the Philippines.

But there were always more challenges around the corner. After Usha's five-gold haul at Jakarta, she was accused of doping. Some people even thought she was a man. Else how could she have won at everything? Usually, tests for doping are conducted only a couple of times, but Usha had to go through the indignity of being tested for drugs after every race. This resulted in delays, and affected her preparations for the next event. But she took that in her stride (pun intended!).

The 1988 Seoul Olympics was just around the corner. Usha thought she was doing well. She'd changed her stride strategy, and she was raring to go and get the medal that she craved for. But then, she injured her heel, and it hampered her training efforts. So, although she did qualify for the Olympics, she didn't even clear the heats at the 400m hurdles.

The same nation that had cheered for her and feted her for her other wins, now turned against her. Her fellow athletes shamed her publicly; people threw stones at her house. Usha locked herself into her room. She didn't talk to anybody. 'I was very, very hurt,' she said. 'That was a period when I hated sports.'

Usha pulled herself out of the dejection. 'I wanted to win, feel happy again,' she said. She was back in good form, and won four golds and two silvers at the Asian Athletics Championships in Delhi in 1989.

Then she decided that it was time to retire.

But the Beijing Asian Games 1990 were around the corner, and officials from the Sports Authority of India pleaded with her to run for the country, and when she refused, sent her a touching letter. So, she went back and won three silver medals, in spite of being ill-prepared.

Immediately after, she announced her retirement and married V Sreenivasan, a CISF inspector and sports enthusiast. They had a son, Ujwal, in 1992.

But India hadn't seen the last of her. After three years, she made a comeback. Usha can't run again, naysayers said. Not after marriage and a child. She has put on weight. She is past her prime.

It didn't affect Usha. She won bronze medals at the Asian Athletics Championships in Fukuoka, Japan in 1998. In 1999, she broke her own 200m national record. And when she retired in 2000, she was still ranked the topmost athlete in India!

Dreams, goals and regrets

Usha came a hair's breadth away from an Olympic medal in spite of having next to no training. She had no exposure. She had no training partners. She had no special diet, took no supplements. In the days leading to her Olympic races, she made do with rice porridge and mango pickle. She had no physiotherapists, no massage experts: 'After every race, I went and had a bath, that's all.'

'If I could get within reach of that Olympic medal without any facilities, then why can't others do it if they have the required facilities?' Usha wondered and that is why she started the Usha School of Athletics near Kozhikode, Kerala in 2002. 'I am convinced that what we lack in India is not talent, but the basic, modern and scientific facilities,' she said.

Usha is confident that 'within the next three Olympics, India will have the first Olympic medal in track and field. Once the first medal comes, more will follow.'

PT Usha's student Tintu Lukka and Jisna Matthew, and other athletes like Hima Das are making waves in the field already. Hima Das has become the first Indian woman to win a gold medal at the world level, when she won at the World Under-20 Athletics Championships at Finland.

While Usha is an inspiration to the new generation of athletes, she still has her own heroes. She likes Usain Bolt's looks and Carl Lewis' acceleration during sprints, and his double jumps in the long jump event. Her hero is Edwin Moses, whom she met for the first time in 1984 at Los Angeles. She had put up his photograph in her room. And she used to watch videos of his hurdle races. She is in awe of the length, strength and confidence of his strides between each hurdle.

Her only lasting regret is that Olympic medal, of course. 'If life could come back, if I could roll back the years, I would like to relive my most cherished moment, the Los Angeles Olympics. I would like to compete with the same fellow runners, but this time finishing at the podium.'

The Indian Olympic Association honoured Usha with the sportsperson of the century award in 1999, and the sports woman of the millennium. She won the Arjuna Award in 1983 and the Padma Shree in 1985.

SOME INDIAN WOMEN AT THE OLYMPICS

The first time Indian women went the Olympics was at Helsinki in 1952. They were athlete **Mary D'Souza**, who ran the 100m and 200m races, hurdler **Nilima Ghose**, and swimmers **Dolly Nazir** and **Arati Saha**.

The first Indian woman Olympic medallist was weightlifter **Karnam Malleshwari**, who bagged the bronze medal in the 2000 Sydney Games.

AROUND THE WORLD

Women participated in Olympics for the first time in the 1900 Paris games, in lawn tennis, golf, sailing, croquet and equestrian events. Only 2.2 per cent of the total participants were women (women now make up 40-50 percent of the participants).

Helene de Pourtales (1868–1945), a sailor, became the first Olympic champion, she and the Swiss team won a sailing event, and won both the gold and the silver medals (it is not clear who else was on the team). The first woman to win an individual Olympic event was **Charlotte Cooper** of UK, in lawn tennis.

Shruthi Rao (shruthi-rao.com) studied to be an energy engineer and worked as a software professional until her story-gobbling-monster-daughter pulled out the writer lurking inside her. She writes for both adults and children, and is a freelance editor. She loves books, science, trees, desserts, hikes and the internet.